HOW IT WORKS
THE
WORLD OF
ANIMAL LIFE

Text by Gerald Legg
Illustrated by Steve Weston

BARNES
& NOBLE
BOOKS
NEW YORK

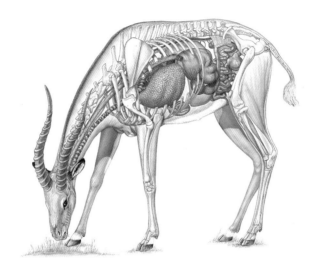

**This edition published by Barnes & Noble, Inc.,
by arrangement with Horus Editions Limited**

Copyright © 1998 Horus Editions Limited

Project manager Jenny Fry
Text editor Helen Maxey
Series editor Elizabeth Miles
Designed by Paul Richards and Steve Weston
Additional illustrations by Ruth Lindsay and David Wright

1998 Barnes & Noble Books

ISBN 0-7607-0908-4

9 8 7 6 5 4 3 2 1 M 98 99 00 01 02 03

Printed in Singapore

HOW IT WORKS

CONTENTS

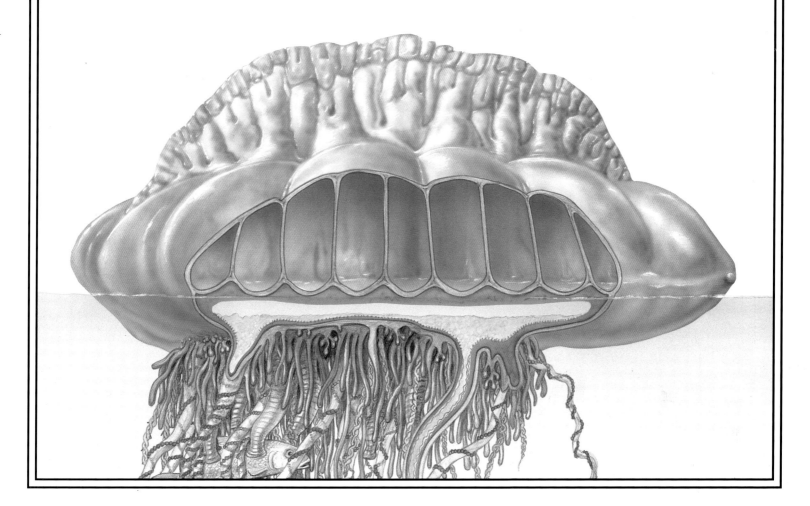

Bony Fish

THIS COLORFUL fish, called an Anthias, is a tropical fish that lives among coral. It is one of the 20,000 different kinds of fish that have a bony skeleton.

To move through water, fish have a special shape. Most have a long body, pointed at the front and narrowing at the tail. It is smooth, without any untidy bits sticking out. However, not all fish are streamlined like this. Some fish that live amongst coral, seaweed, or on the sea bed move differently, so they need a different body shape.

Some fish hunt, while others scavenge, eating up dead material that is floating around. To feed, many fish approach their meal and quickly open their mouth when they are close to it. This movement of the bones around the mouth and gills opens up the throat. Water rushes in, bringing the food with it.

EEL

FLYING FISH

SEAHORSE

ANGEL FISH

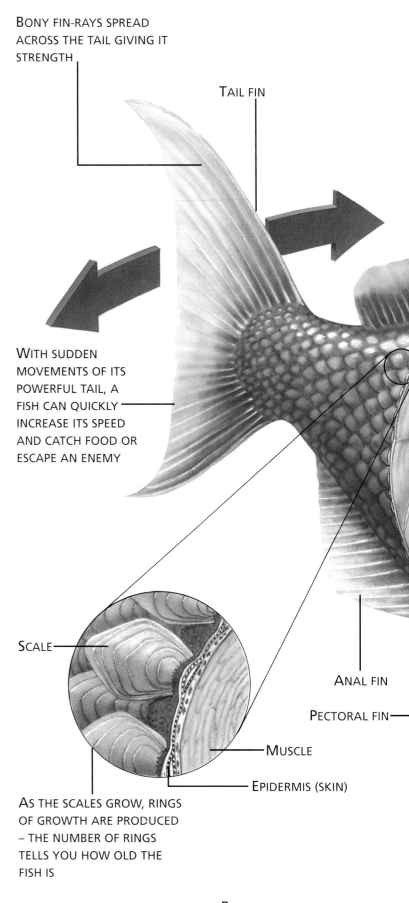

BONY FIN-RAYS SPREAD ACROSS THE TAIL GIVING IT STRENGTH

TAIL FIN

WITH SUDDEN MOVEMENTS OF ITS POWERFUL TAIL, A FISH CAN QUICKLY INCREASE ITS SPEED AND CATCH FOOD OR ESCAPE AN ENEMY

SCALE

MUSCLE

EPIDERMIS (SKIN)

ANAL FIN

PECTORAL FIN

AS THE SCALES GROW, RINGS OF GROWTH ARE PRODUCED – THE NUMBER OF RINGS TELLS YOU HOW OLD THE FISH IS

PELVIC AND PECTORAL FINS STEER THE FISH, MOVE IT UP AND DOWN IN THE WATER, AND ALSO ACT AS BRAKES

Fins

Fish use their fins in all kinds of ways. Eels have a long dorsal fin that ripples, gently propelling them along the sea bottom. Flying fish have big wing-like fins on their chest (pectoral fins). Angel fish use their fins to dart in and out of their coral hideouts. Seahorses have a fin on their back (the dorsal fin) that enables them to hover and move delicately through seaweed.

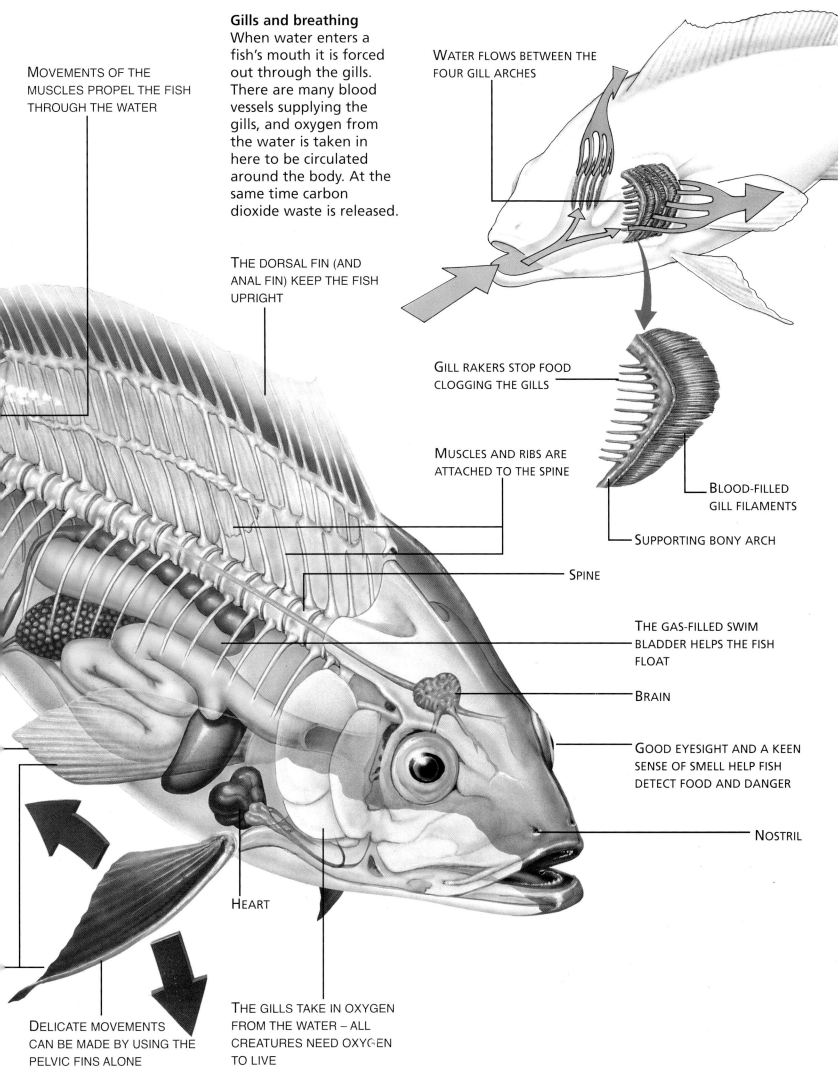

MOVEMENTS OF THE MUSCLES PROPEL THE FISH THROUGH THE WATER

Gills and breathing
When water enters a fish's mouth it is forced out through the gills. There are many blood vessels supplying the gills, and oxygen from the water is taken in here to be circulated around the body. At the same time carbon dioxide waste is released.

WATER FLOWS BETWEEN THE FOUR GILL ARCHES

THE DORSAL FIN (AND ANAL FIN) KEEP THE FISH UPRIGHT

GILL RAKERS STOP FOOD CLOGGING THE GILLS

MUSCLES AND RIBS ARE ATTACHED TO THE SPINE

BLOOD-FILLED GILL FILAMENTS

SUPPORTING BONY ARCH

SPINE

THE GAS-FILLED SWIM BLADDER HELPS THE FISH FLOAT

BRAIN

GOOD EYESIGHT AND A KEEN SENSE OF SMELL HELP FISH DETECT FOOD AND DANGER

NOSTRIL

HEART

DELICATE MOVEMENTS CAN BE MADE BY USING THE PELVIC FINS ALONE

THE GILLS TAKE IN OXYGEN FROM THE WATER – ALL CREATURES NEED OXYGEN TO LIVE

Bird Flight

THE OSPREY is a bird of prey. It flies over rivers, lakes, and seas hunting for fish. On spotting a fish it can make a dramatic dive, feet-first, into the water. After grabbing its prey, the hawk-like bird will soar up into the sky.

Like all birds, to push its body upwards, the osprey must beat its wings downwards against the air. The wings of a bird have a special curved shape (airfoil) which produces lift and keeps the bird in the air as it flies. The wing-shape also means birds can glide or soar on rising currents of air. Birds hardly need to beat their wings if they can 'ride' on a wind that is flowing upwards over a hill. A bird steers itself by changing the tilt of its wings, or by twisting its tail like a rudder.

THE 'WRIST' BONES ARE FLEXIBLE SO THE WINGS CAN BE TILTED, ALLOWING THE BIRD TO TWIST AND TURN IN FLIGHT

THE PRIMARY FEATHERS ARE THE MAIN FLIGHT FEATHERS

THE SECONDARY FEATHERS GIVE THE WING A LARGE SURFACE AREA

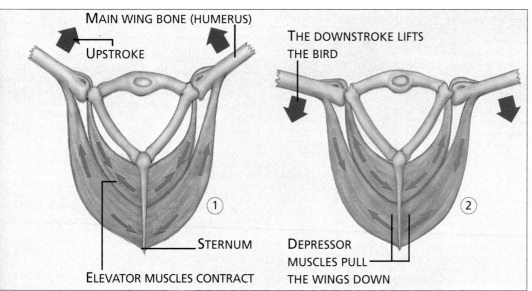

MAIN WING BONE (HUMERUS)

UPSTROKE

THE DOWNSTROKE LIFTS THE BIRD

① STERNUM

ELEVATOR MUSCLES CONTRACT

DEPRESSOR MUSCLES PULL THE WINGS DOWN

②

BROAD TAIL FEATHERS ACT LIKE A RUDDER FOR STEERING THE BIRD

THE SHARP, CLAWED TOES ARE CALLED TALONS

A bird's wingbeat

To fly through the air, or hover, a bird must beat its wings. A pair of large breast muscles make each wing move. For an upward stroke (1) the depressor muscles relax (lengthen) and the elevator muscles contract (shorten). Like a pulley, this lifts the wing bones. For a downward stroke (2), to lift the bird, the bigger, stronger depressor muscles must contract to pull the wing bones down.

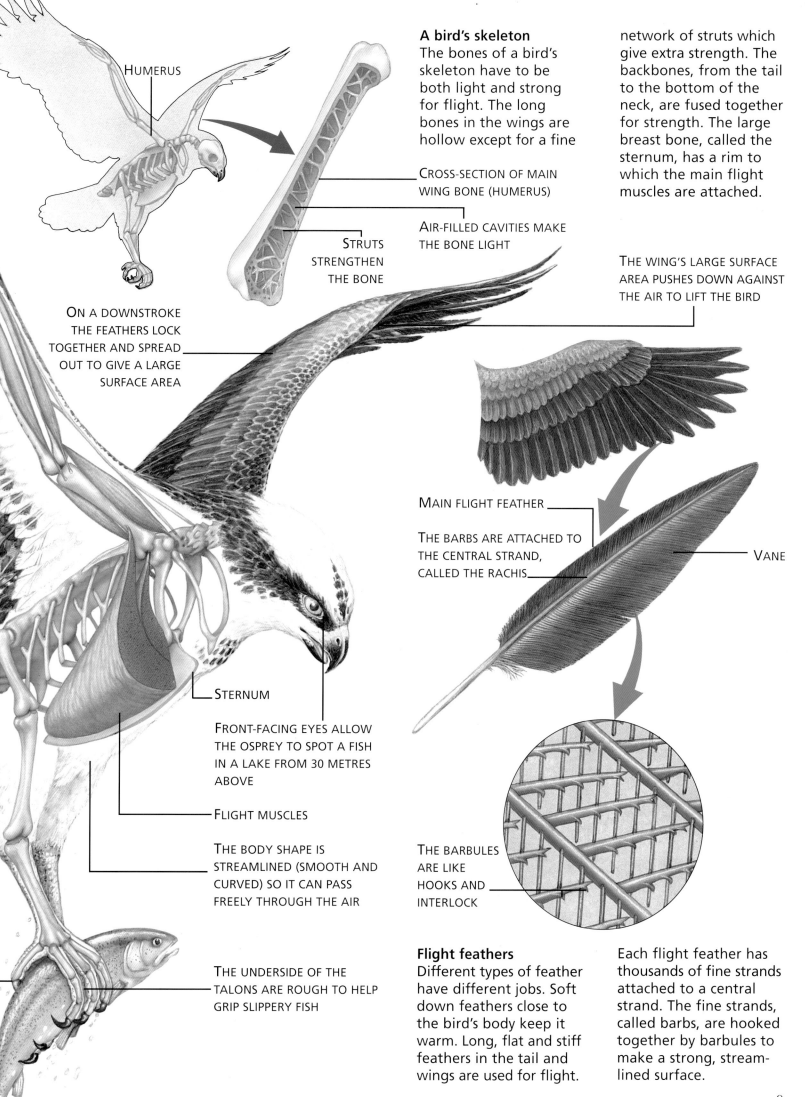

HUMERUS

A bird's skeleton
The bones of a bird's skeleton have to be both light and strong for flight. The long bones in the wings are hollow except for a fine network of struts which give extra strength. The backbones, from the tail to the bottom of the neck, are fused together for strength. The large breast bone, called the sternum, has a rim to which the main flight muscles are attached.

CROSS-SECTION OF MAIN WING BONE (HUMERUS)

AIR-FILLED CAVITIES MAKE THE BONE LIGHT

STRUTS STRENGTHEN THE BONE

ON A DOWNSTROKE THE FEATHERS LOCK TOGETHER AND SPREAD OUT TO GIVE A LARGE SURFACE AREA

THE WING'S LARGE SURFACE AREA PUSHES DOWN AGAINST THE AIR TO LIFT THE BIRD

MAIN FLIGHT FEATHER

THE BARBS ARE ATTACHED TO THE CENTRAL STRAND, CALLED THE RACHIS

VANE

STERNUM

FRONT-FACING EYES ALLOW THE OSPREY TO SPOT A FISH IN A LAKE FROM 30 METRES ABOVE

FLIGHT MUSCLES

THE BODY SHAPE IS STREAMLINED (SMOOTH AND CURVED) SO IT CAN PASS FREELY THROUGH THE AIR

THE BARBULES ARE LIKE HOOKS AND INTERLOCK

THE UNDERSIDE OF THE TALONS ARE ROUGH TO HELP GRIP SLIPPERY FISH

Flight feathers
Different types of feather have different jobs. Soft down feathers close to the bird's body keep it warm. Long, flat and stiff feathers in the tail and wings are used for flight.

Each flight feather has thousands of fine strands attached to a central strand. The fine strands, called barbs, are hooked together by barbules to make a strong, stream-lined surface.

Seeing with Sound

LAND ANIMALS that are active during daylight use their eyes to see. But how do creatures that move around in the dark see? Marine animals that live in the dark ocean depths and nocturnal land animals that move around at night have a special way of 'seeing'. They use a system called echolocation which allows them to build up a 'sound picture' of everything around them. Most bats use echolocation. The bats make a series of short, sharp sounds. The sounds bounce off objects in their path. Then the bats pick up the echoes (returning sounds) and can tell if an object is moving, how far away it is, and what it is made of.

LONG, THIN FINGER BONES SUPPORT THE WING

A MEMBRANE OF ELASTIC SKIN STRETCHES BETWEEN THE FINGER AND ARM BONES TO FORM THE WING

THE RIBS PROTECT THE LUNGS, HEART, LIVER, AND STOMACH

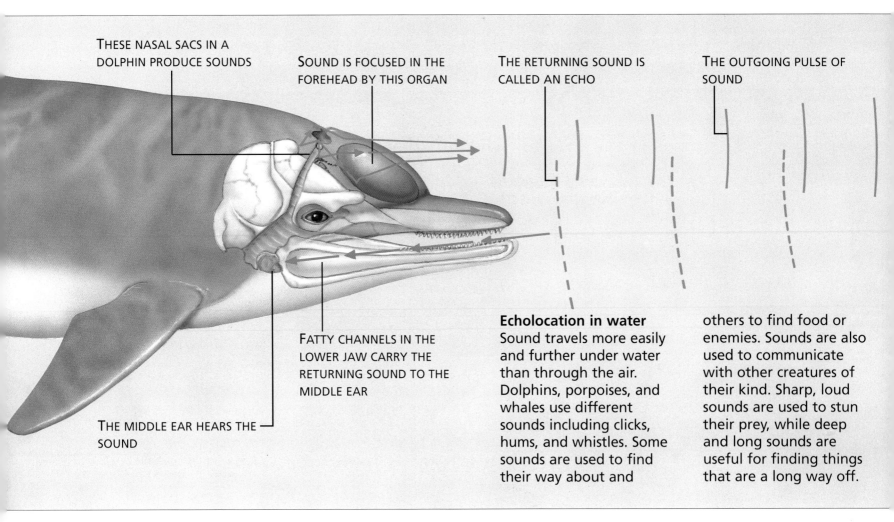

THESE NASAL SACS IN A DOLPHIN PRODUCE SOUNDS

SOUND IS FOCUSED IN THE FOREHEAD BY THIS ORGAN

THE RETURNING SOUND IS CALLED AN ECHO

THE OUTGOING PULSE OF SOUND

FATTY CHANNELS IN THE LOWER JAW CARRY THE RETURNING SOUND TO THE MIDDLE EAR

THE MIDDLE EAR HEARS THE SOUND

Echolocation in water
Sound travels more easily and further under water than through the air. Dolphins, porpoises, and whales use different sounds including clicks, hums, and whistles. Some sounds are used to find their way about and others to find food or enemies. Sounds are also used to communicate with other creatures of their kind. Sharp, loud sounds are used to stun their prey, while deep and long sounds are useful for finding things that are a long way off.

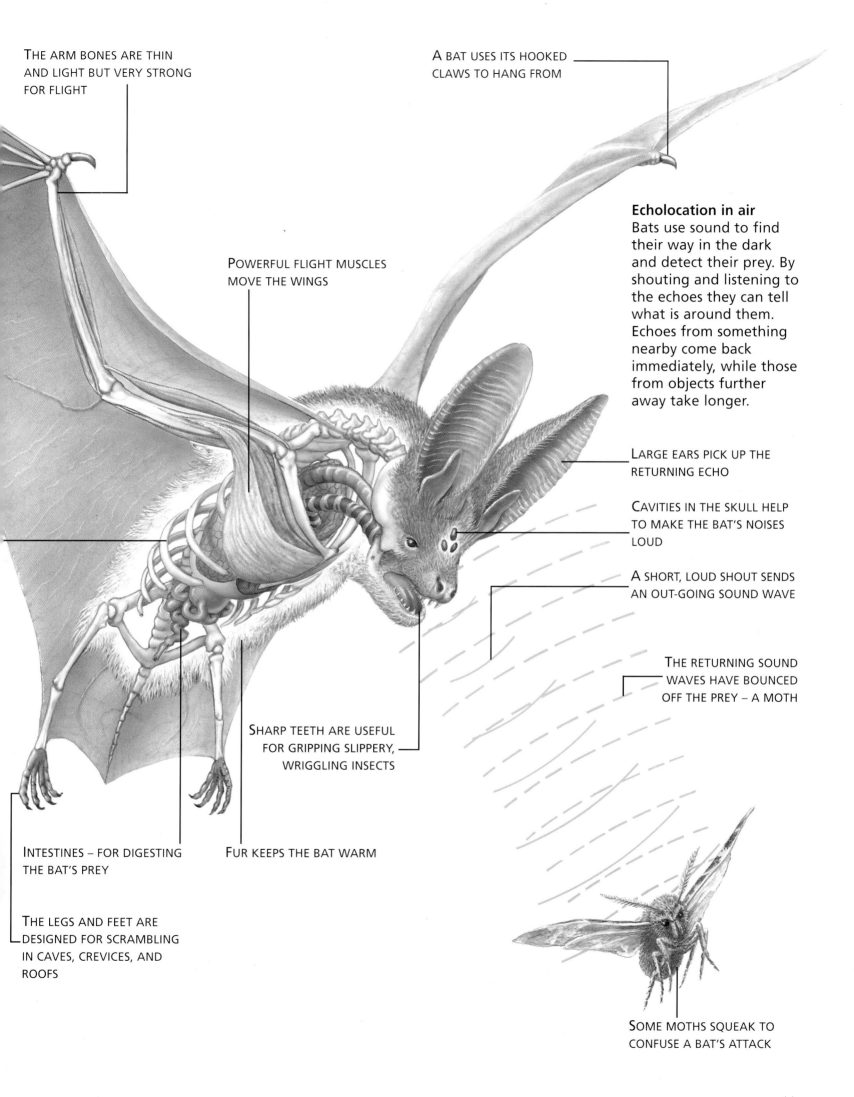

THE ARM BONES ARE THIN AND LIGHT BUT VERY STRONG FOR FLIGHT

A BAT USES ITS HOOKED CLAWS TO HANG FROM

POWERFUL FLIGHT MUSCLES MOVE THE WINGS

Echolocation in air
Bats use sound to find their way in the dark and detect their prey. By shouting and listening to the echoes they can tell what is around them. Echoes from something nearby come back immediately, while those from objects further away take longer.

LARGE EARS PICK UP THE RETURNING ECHO

CAVITIES IN THE SKULL HELP TO MAKE THE BAT'S NOISES LOUD

A SHORT, LOUD SHOUT SENDS AN OUT-GOING SOUND WAVE

THE RETURNING SOUND WAVES HAVE BOUNCED OFF THE PREY – A MOTH

SHARP TEETH ARE USEFUL FOR GRIPPING SLIPPERY, WRIGGLING INSECTS

INTESTINES – FOR DIGESTING THE BAT'S PREY

FUR KEEPS THE BAT WARM

THE LEGS AND FEET ARE DESIGNED FOR SCRAMBLING IN CAVES, CREVICES, AND ROOFS

SOME MOTHS SQUEAK TO CONFUSE A BAT'S ATTACK

A Spider's Web

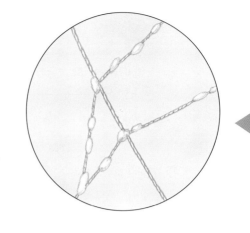

A PREDATOR IS an animal that hunts and kills other animals to feed itself. The garden spider is a predator that spins a web to catch its prey. During late summer the large webs of adult spiders can be found amongst low plants and bushes. Sitting upside-down in the center of the web the spider waits for insects to blunder into its web. It then rushes across, seizing and killing its victim.

If frightened by a bird, which might eat it, the spider will run to safety. It may hide under a leaf or drop to the ground on a silken safety line, the thread that trails from its body so that it never loses contact with its web. Spiders also use their silk to wrap and protect their eggs.

Sticky beads
The spider uses a special silk for trapping insects. At first this silk is coated in a sticky layer. As the silk is fixed to the web's thread, the spider uses its back legs to twang the thread like a guitar string. This breaks the coat into a series of sticky beads.

SPIDERS HAVE FOUR PAIRS OF SEVEN-JOINTED LEGS

THE SUCKING STOMACH DRAWS FOOD INTO THE INTESTINE AND MOUTH HAIRS TRAP ANY SOLID PARTICLES

VENOM (POISON) FROM THIS SAC IS INJECTED INTO THE SPIDER'S PREY TO SUBDUE AND KILL IT

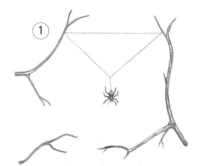

AS IT DANGLES ON THE LINE THE SPIDER SPINS A Y-FORK (1)

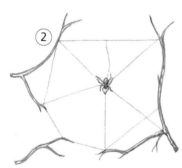

IT ADDS MORE SPOKES TO THE WHEEL TO MAKE A STRONG WEB (2)

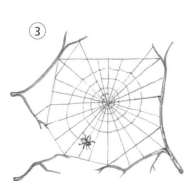

A SUPPORTING SPIRAL IS LAID DOWN BEFORE THE FINAL STICKY SPIRAL (3)

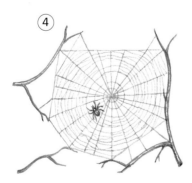

THE WEB IS COMPLETE AND READY FOR CATCHING INSECTS (4)

Web spinning
To begin its web the spider either floats its silk across a gap so the silk catches on the other side or it walks around trailing the silk behind it. The silken rope is then pulled tight and fixed. Climbing across this line, the spider lays down a stronger one. A loose loop is spun and a Y-shaped fork is created. More spokes are added to help the spider walk across the web and wind its thread round in a spiral. The spider uses its long legs to keep the web an even shape as it spins.

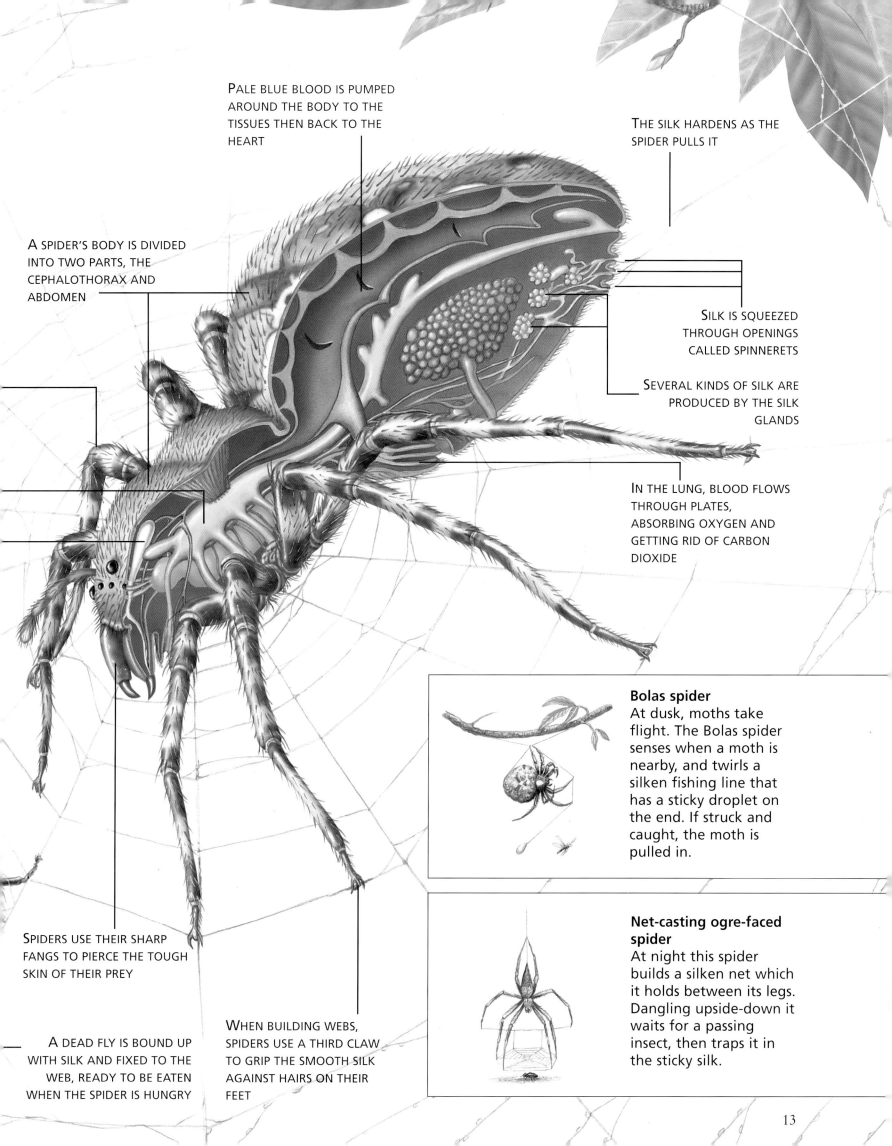

PALE BLUE BLOOD IS PUMPED AROUND THE BODY TO THE TISSUES THEN BACK TO THE HEART

THE SILK HARDENS AS THE SPIDER PULLS IT

A SPIDER'S BODY IS DIVIDED INTO TWO PARTS, THE CEPHALOTHORAX AND ABDOMEN

SILK IS SQUEEZED THROUGH OPENINGS CALLED SPINNERETS

SEVERAL KINDS OF SILK ARE PRODUCED BY THE SILK GLANDS

IN THE LUNG, BLOOD FLOWS THROUGH PLATES, ABSORBING OXYGEN AND GETTING RID OF CARBON DIOXIDE

SPIDERS USE THEIR SHARP FANGS TO PIERCE THE TOUGH SKIN OF THEIR PREY

A DEAD FLY IS BOUND UP WITH SILK AND FIXED TO THE WEB, READY TO BE EATEN WHEN THE SPIDER IS HUNGRY

WHEN BUILDING WEBS, SPIDERS USE A THIRD CLAW TO GRIP THE SMOOTH SILK AGAINST HAIRS ON THEIR FEET

Bolas spider
At dusk, moths take flight. The Bolas spider senses when a moth is nearby, and twirls a silken fishing line that has a sticky droplet on the end. If struck and caught, the moth is pulled in.

Net-casting ogre-faced spider
At night this spider builds a silken net which it holds between its legs. Dangling upside-down it waits for a passing insect, then traps it in the sticky silk.

Grazing Animals

IMPALA ARE large grazing antelope found in the savanna woodlands and grasslands of Africa. They live in herds of ten to several hundred individuals. Each herd is led by one of the older males. Younger males act as guards. If they are frightened by another animal, such as a lion, they make a sneezing sound to warn the others, and then the herd bounds away.

An impala can get a good hold on plants and grass by wrapping its long tongue around them. Their sharp incisors (front teeth) bite off blades of grass and plant shoots to eat. The molars (back teeth) have large flattened tops which are ideal for grinding grass. Grass is difficult to digest (break down) and to get enough food impalas have to eat a lot of grass. They eat quickly and then retire to digest it in safety, chewing it a second time. This system of digestion is called rumination.

A four-part stomach
Swallowed food passes into the rumen (1) where it is broken down into small balls of cud. The cud is returned to the mouth for more chewing. Once swallowed again, the food is digested back in the rumen (1), then the reticulum (2). Next, water is squeezed from the food in the omasum (3) and further digested in the abomasum (4) before passing into the intestines.

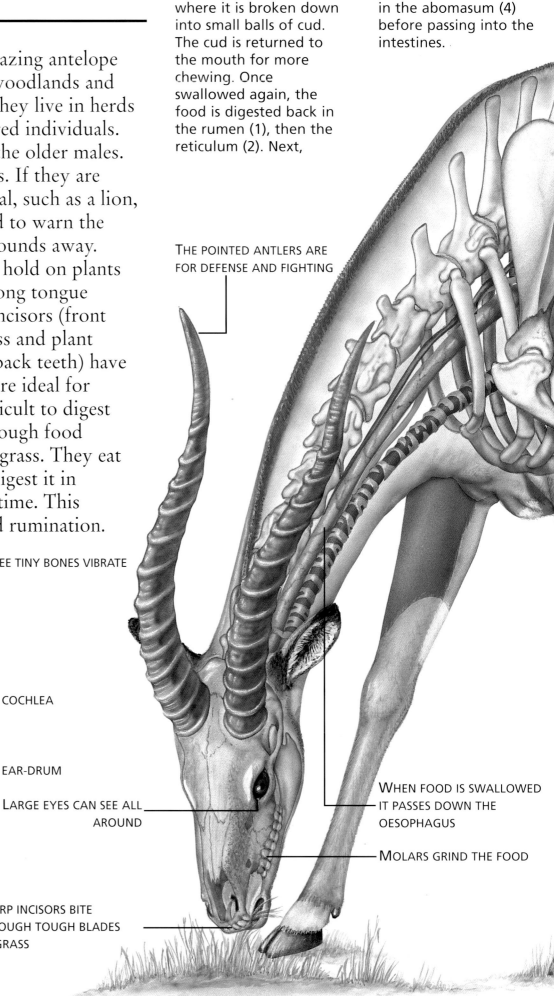

THE POINTED ANTLERS ARE FOR DEFENSE AND FIGHTING

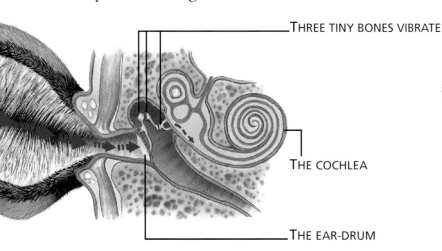

THREE TINY BONES VIBRATE

THE COCHLEA

THE EAR-DRUM

Listening for danger
Impalas' ears listen for danger. Sound travels into the ear and vibrates the ear-drum. This moves three tiny bones, which in turn move a membrane (thin tissue) causing the liquid in the cochlea to move. This triggers tiny hairs which send signals to the brain.

LARGE EYES CAN SEE ALL AROUND

SHARP INCISORS BITE THROUGH TOUGH BLADES OF GRASS

WHEN FOOD IS SWALLOWED IT PASSES DOWN THE OESOPHAGUS

MOLARS GRIND THE FOOD

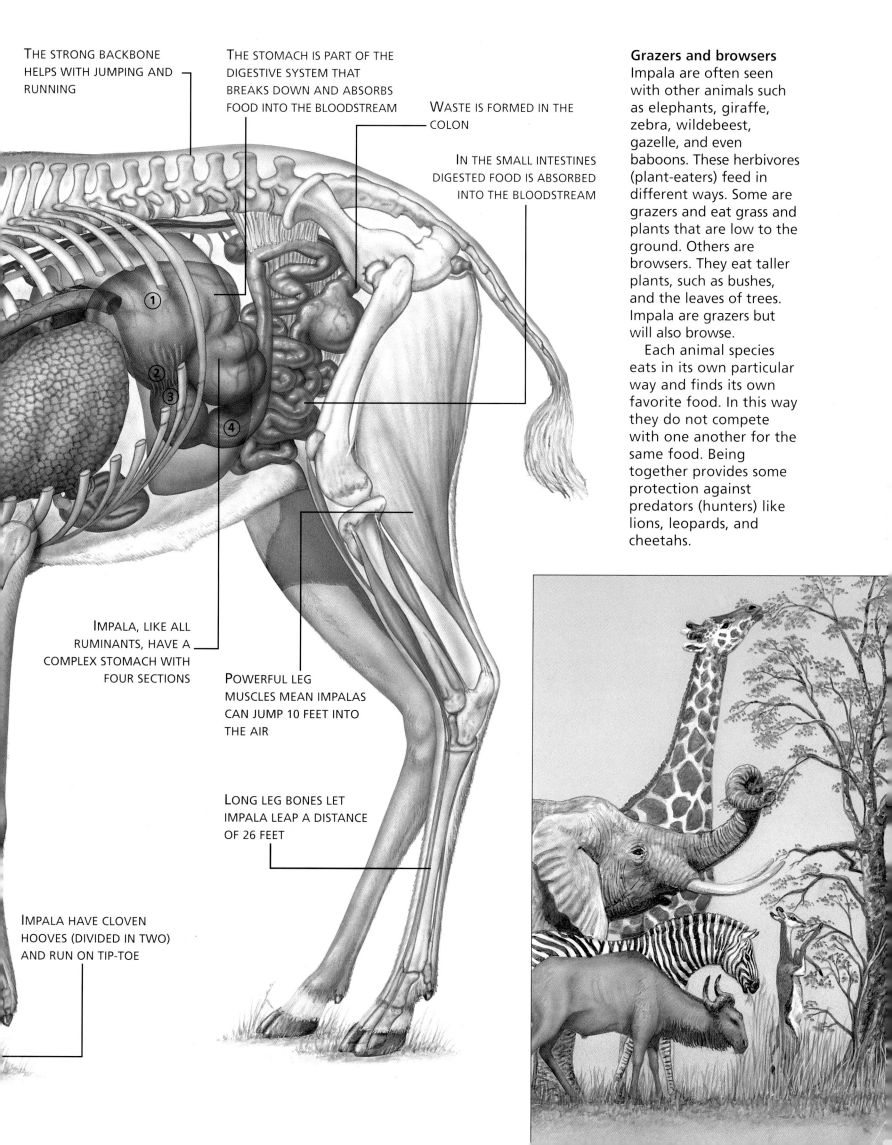

THE STRONG BACKBONE HELPS WITH JUMPING AND RUNNING

THE STOMACH IS PART OF THE DIGESTIVE SYSTEM THAT BREAKS DOWN AND ABSORBS FOOD INTO THE BLOODSTREAM

WASTE IS FORMED IN THE COLON

IN THE SMALL INTESTINES DIGESTED FOOD IS ABSORBED INTO THE BLOODSTREAM

IMPALA, LIKE ALL RUMINANTS, HAVE A COMPLEX STOMACH WITH FOUR SECTIONS

POWERFUL LEG MUSCLES MEAN IMPALAS CAN JUMP 10 FEET INTO THE AIR

LONG LEG BONES LET IMPALA LEAP A DISTANCE OF 26 FEET

IMPALA HAVE CLOVEN HOOVES (DIVIDED IN TWO) AND RUN ON TIP-TOE

Grazers and browsers
Impala are often seen with other animals such as elephants, giraffe, zebra, wildebeest, gazelle, and even baboons. These herbivores (plant-eaters) feed in different ways. Some are grazers and eat grass and plants that are low to the ground. Others are browsers. They eat taller plants, such as bushes, and the leaves of trees. Impala are grazers but will also browse.

Each animal species eats in its own particular way and finds its own favorite food. In this way they do not compete with one another for the same food. Being together provides some protection against predators (hunters) like lions, leopards, and cheetahs.

Hunters

HUNTING ANIMALS have special features and skills for catching their prey. The big cats, including the lion, tiger, leopard, jaguar, and cheetah (*right*), hunt the largest animals. They have to be clever, fast, and strong to catch them. Their jaws are short and strong, and they have a powerful skull and large sharp teeth so that they can quickly tear their prey apart. They use their long canine teeth to stab their victims and chisel-like incisors to nip through tough skin. They also have razor-sharp chewing teeth which slice quickly through flesh.

Of all the cats the cheetah is the best known for its hunting ability. It can reach 60 miles per hour, making it the fastest animal on four legs. Its slim body is designed for speed.

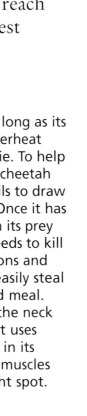

A LONG TAIL HELPS WITH BALANCE WHEN RUNNING AT SPEED

STRONG BONES SUPPORT THE LONG, FLEXIBLE TAIL

POWERFUL LEG MUSCLES DRIVE THE CHEETAH AT HIGH SPEEDS

ITS LONG LEG BONES HELP IT COVER DISTANCE QUICKLY

A STRONG ACHILLES TENDON JOINS THE CALF MUSCLES TO THE HEEL

LARGE ANKLE BONES (HEELS) STRENGTHEN THE JOINTS FOR LANDING

LONG LOWER LEG BONES HELP THE CHEETAH TO RUN FAST

Hunting

Cheetahs have special features which help them hunt. Their eyes are designed to detect moving prey against the horizon. Hiding in the grass, the cheetah selects its victims. Young gazelle are chased when they are as much as 1,640 feet away; adult gazelle, who are more alert, are chased when they are up to 164 feet away. A cheetah cannot run at high speed for long as its body would overheat and it would die. To help it cool off, the cheetah has wide nostrils to draw in cooling air. Once it has caught up with its prey the cheetah needs to kill it quickly, as lions and hyenas could easily steal its hard-earned meal. When it bites the neck of small prey, it uses special sensors in its teeth and jaw muscles to find the right spot.

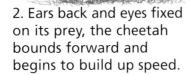

The chase
1. The cheetah stalks its victim before beginning its high-speed chase.

2. Ears back and eyes fixed on its prey, the cheetah bounds forward and begins to build up speed.

3. Its prey spots the cheetah and runs fast to escape, but the cheetah races after it. The cheetah matches the prey's speed and movements before trying to knock it over.

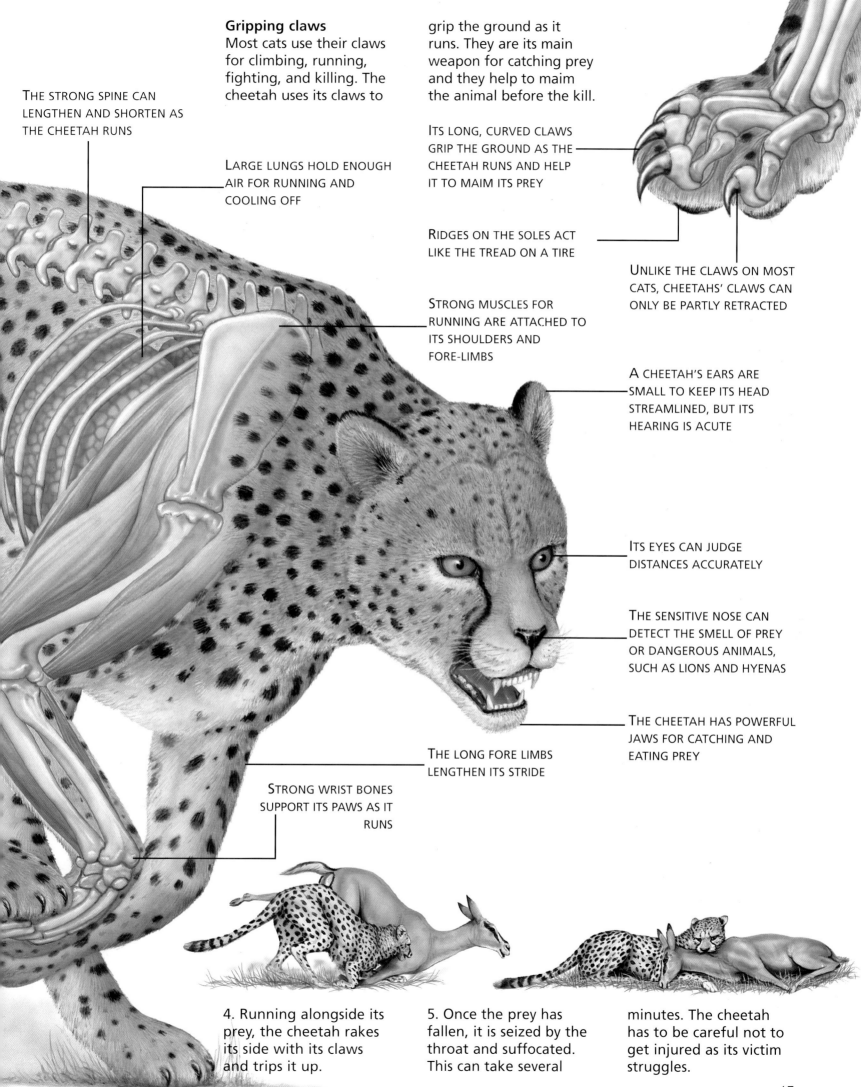

Gripping claws
Most cats use their claws for climbing, running, fighting, and killing. The cheetah uses its claws to grip the ground as it runs. They are its main weapon for catching prey and they help to maim the animal before the kill.

THE STRONG SPINE CAN LENGTHEN AND SHORTEN AS THE CHEETAH RUNS

LARGE LUNGS HOLD ENOUGH AIR FOR RUNNING AND COOLING OFF

ITS LONG, CURVED CLAWS GRIP THE GROUND AS THE CHEETAH RUNS AND HELP IT TO MAIM ITS PREY

RIDGES ON THE SOLES ACT LIKE THE TREAD ON A TIRE

UNLIKE THE CLAWS ON MOST CATS, CHEETAHS' CLAWS CAN ONLY BE PARTLY RETRACTED

STRONG MUSCLES FOR RUNNING ARE ATTACHED TO ITS SHOULDERS AND FORE-LIMBS

A CHEETAH'S EARS ARE SMALL TO KEEP ITS HEAD STREAMLINED, BUT ITS HEARING IS ACUTE

ITS EYES CAN JUDGE DISTANCES ACCURATELY

THE SENSITIVE NOSE CAN DETECT THE SMELL OF PREY OR DANGEROUS ANIMALS, SUCH AS LIONS AND HYENAS

THE CHEETAH HAS POWERFUL JAWS FOR CATCHING AND EATING PREY

THE LONG FORE LIMBS LENGTHEN ITS STRIDE

STRONG WRIST BONES SUPPORT ITS PAWS AS IT RUNS

4. Running alongside its prey, the cheetah rakes its side with its claws and trips it up.

5. Once the prey has fallen, it is seized by the throat and suffocated. This can take several minutes. The cheetah has to be careful not to get injured as its victim struggles.

17

Snakes

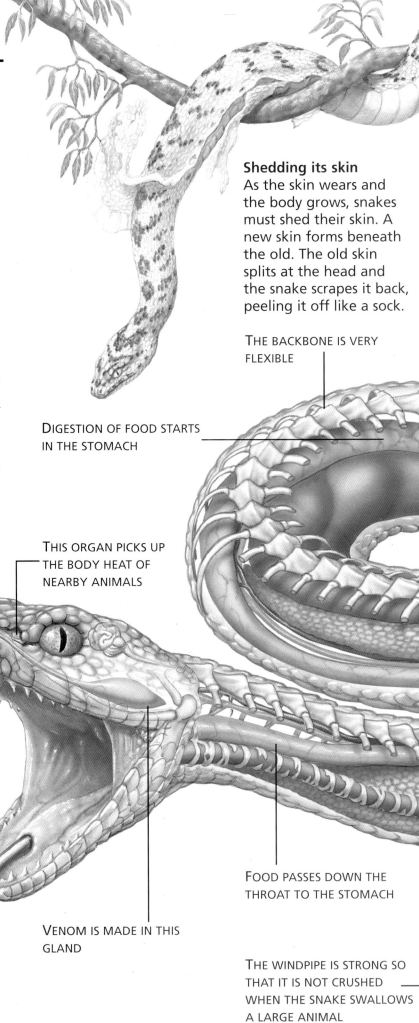

THIS SNAKE is called a green bamboo tree viper. It comes from southeast Asia and can grow up to 3 feet in length. It lives in trees which it can easily climb using a strong tail and rough scales to grasp the twigs and leaves. The viper feeds on small mammals, birds, lizards, and frogs. When baby vipers are born about a dozen appear at a time. Before they are born baby vipers hatch out of their eggs while the eggs are still inside their mother's body.

Because snakes do not have arms or legs to help them catch their food, many have venom (poison) instead. The venom can kill the live animal so that it is ready to eat. Some snakes do not use venom. Instead they feed on prey that is too slow or too small to escape. They either grab and eat it quickly, or coil their bodies around it and suffocate it.

Shedding its skin
As the skin wears and the body grows, snakes must shed their skin. A new skin forms beneath the old. The old skin splits at the head and the snake scrapes it back, peeling it off like a sock.

THE BACKBONE IS VERY FLEXIBLE

DIGESTION OF FOOD STARTS IN THE STOMACH

CLOSED MOUTH

THE FANGS ARE TUCKED INSIDE

OPEN MOUTH

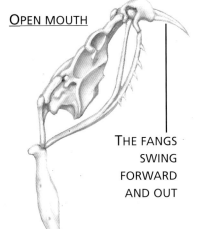

THE FANGS SWING FORWARD AND OUT

VENOM FROM THE POISON GLANDS IS INJECTED THROUGH THE SYRINGE-LIKE FANGS

THE FORKED TONGUE CAN 'TASTE' ANY SMELLS IN THE AIR

THIS ORGAN PICKS UP THE BODY HEAT OF NEARBY ANIMALS

VENOM IS MADE IN THIS GLAND

FOOD PASSES DOWN THE THROAT TO THE STOMACH

THE WINDPIPE IS STRONG SO THAT IT IS NOT CRUSHED WHEN THE SNAKE SWALLOWS A LARGE ANIMAL

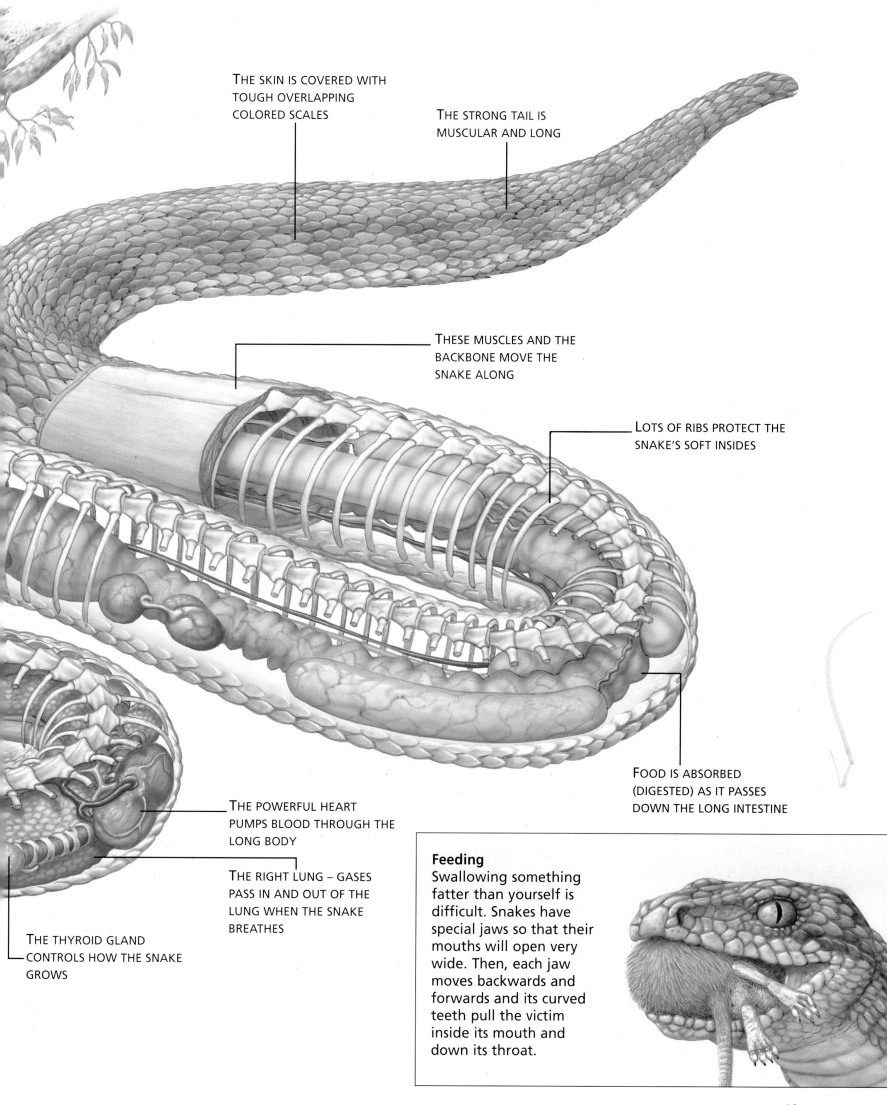

THE SKIN IS COVERED WITH TOUGH OVERLAPPING COLORED SCALES

THE STRONG TAIL IS MUSCULAR AND LONG

THESE MUSCLES AND THE BACKBONE MOVE THE SNAKE ALONG

LOTS OF RIBS PROTECT THE SNAKE'S SOFT INSIDES

FOOD IS ABSORBED (DIGESTED) AS IT PASSES DOWN THE LONG INTESTINE

THE POWERFUL HEART PUMPS BLOOD THROUGH THE LONG BODY

THE RIGHT LUNG – GASES PASS IN AND OUT OF THE LUNG WHEN THE SNAKE BREATHES

THE THYROID GLAND CONTROLS HOW THE SNAKE GROWS

Feeding
Swallowing something fatter than yourself is difficult. Snakes have special jaws so that their mouths will open very wide. Then, each jaw moves backwards and forwards and its curved teeth pull the victim inside its mouth and down its throat.

Sea Mammals

WHALES, SEALS, and sealions are all marine (sea-dwelling) mammals. Being mammals they are warm-blooded, breathe air, and give birth to live young who are suckled on milk produced by their mother. Seals and sealions do not live in the sea all the time. They come ashore to rest and rear their young. Whales spend all their life in the sea and never go on land except accidentally, if they become stranded.

Whales are perfectly designed for their ocean life. They are smooth, streamlined and have a powerful tail, making them excellent swimmers. They often dive to depths where there is no light, but they know where they are by using sound. This system of 'seeing' is called echolocation (see pages 10–11).

Blowhole
A whale's nostrils are on top of its head. They close up when the whale travels downwards. As it surfaces, waste air in the lungs expands and is forced out of the blowhole.

AS THE WHALE SURFACES, AIR IN THE LUNGS EXPANDS AND IS FORCED OUT

THE BLOWHOLE IS CLOSED AS THE WHALE SWIMS UNDERWATER

A HUMPBACK WHALE CAN WEIGH UP TO 80 TONS

CROSS-SECTIONS OF A WHALE'S BLOWHOLE

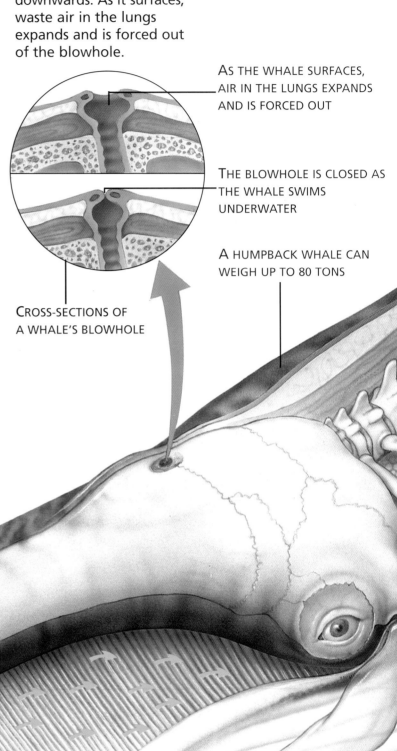

HORNY KNOBS OF SKIN ARE HOME TO WORMS AND OTHER CREATURES

THE BALEEN ARE ATTACHED TO THE UPPER JAW

Baleen
Hard brush-like plates, called baleen, hang down inside the whale's mouth. Each of the hundreds of plates are covered in fine bristles. As its mouth opens, water floods in, sometimes carrying with it the whale's favorite food of tiny shrimp-like creatures called krill. When its mouth closes, the water is forced out through the bristles, trapping the krill.

THE TONGUE SQUEEZES WATER FROM THE MOUTH, SCRAPES THE KRILL FROM THE BALEEN, AND PUSHES IT DOWN THE THROAT

THE JAWS OPEN VERY WIDE WHEN IT FEEDS

PLEATS (FOLDS IN THE SKIN) UNFOLD AS THE MOUTH FILLS WITH WATER

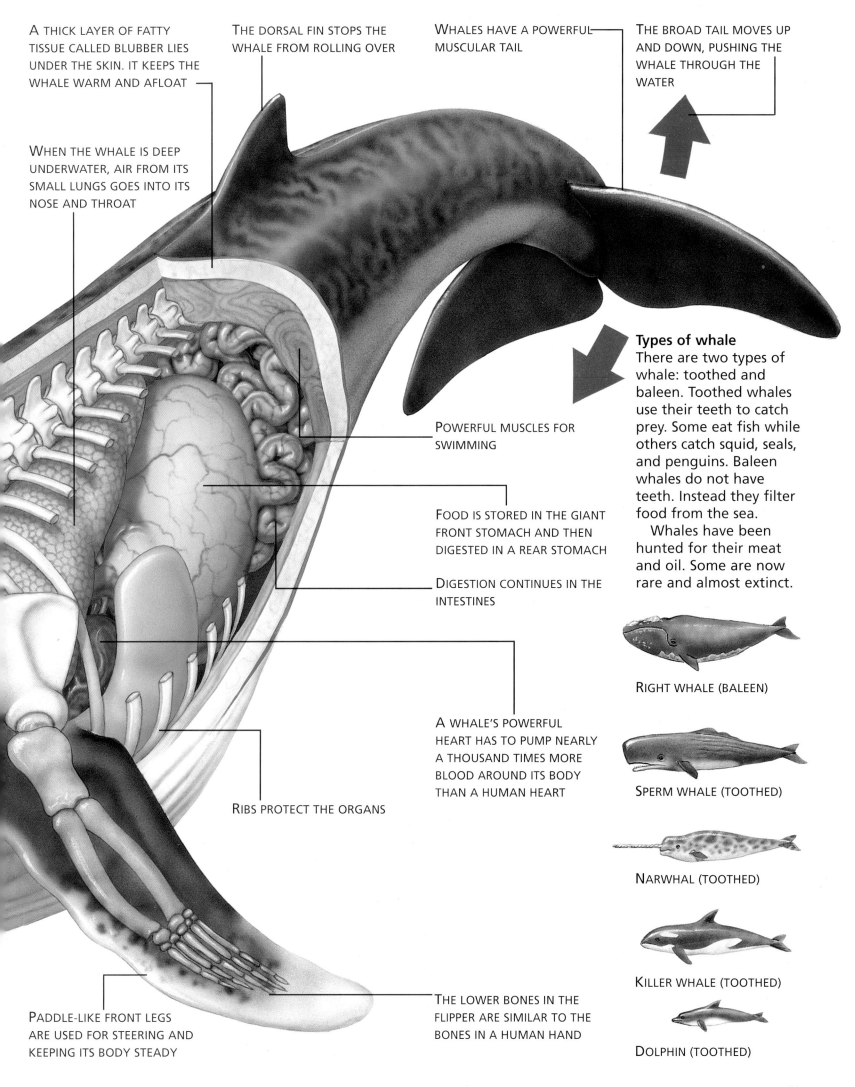

A THICK LAYER OF FATTY TISSUE CALLED BLUBBER LIES UNDER THE SKIN. IT KEEPS THE WHALE WARM AND AFLOAT

THE DORSAL FIN STOPS THE WHALE FROM ROLLING OVER

WHALES HAVE A POWERFUL MUSCULAR TAIL

THE BROAD TAIL MOVES UP AND DOWN, PUSHING THE WHALE THROUGH THE WATER

WHEN THE WHALE IS DEEP UNDERWATER, AIR FROM ITS SMALL LUNGS GOES INTO ITS NOSE AND THROAT

POWERFUL MUSCLES FOR SWIMMING

FOOD IS STORED IN THE GIANT FRONT STOMACH AND THEN DIGESTED IN A REAR STOMACH

DIGESTION CONTINUES IN THE INTESTINES

A WHALE'S POWERFUL HEART HAS TO PUMP NEARLY A THOUSAND TIMES MORE BLOOD AROUND ITS BODY THAN A HUMAN HEART

RIBS PROTECT THE ORGANS

PADDLE-LIKE FRONT LEGS ARE USED FOR STEERING AND KEEPING ITS BODY STEADY

THE LOWER BONES IN THE FLIPPER ARE SIMILAR TO THE BONES IN A HUMAN HAND

Types of whale
There are two types of whale: toothed and baleen. Toothed whales use their teeth to catch prey. Some eat fish while others catch squid, seals, and penguins. Baleen whales do not have teeth. Instead they filter food from the sea.

Whales have been hunted for their meat and oil. Some are now rare and almost extinct.

RIGHT WHALE (BALEEN)

SPERM WHALE (TOOTHED)

NARWHAL (TOOTHED)

KILLER WHALE (TOOTHED)

DOLPHIN (TOOTHED)

Self-defense

ANIMALS HAVE to defend themselves against attack. They do this in different ways. Some use violence and they may be big and fierce, armed with sharp teeth, poison, or strong claws. Gentle animals like antelope can also be violent, using their antlers to fight off an enemy. A few creatures use special defenses. Porcupines have spines, camels spit, and bees sting. Disguise can also be used for self-protection. Some animals use color and the shape of their body to disguise themselves. This defense is called camouflage. They are colored to match their surroundings, making them invisible to predators. Some look like leaves, others like stones. Their coloring can also act as a warning, signalling that they are poisonous or dangerous.

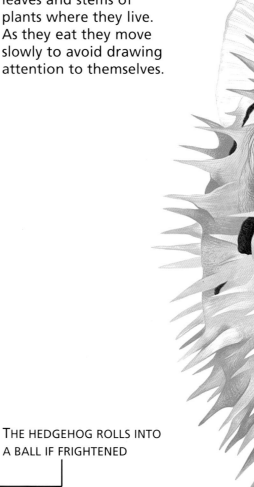

Insect camouflage
Insects are often camouflaged to match their surroundings. They hide away amongst the leaves and stems of plants where they live. As they eat they move slowly to avoid drawing attention to themselves.

THE LANTERN BUG MATCHES THE COLOR OF THE LEAVES

A prickly ball
Hedgehogs are bold and move about noisily at night, hunting for worms, insects, snails, and even small snakes. They can do this because they are protected from most predators by stiff spines on their back and sides. The spines are in fact hollow, sharp hairs. If frightened a hedgehog rolls up into a tight prickly ball as its muscles contract (shorten).

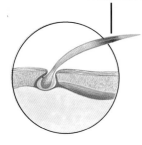

THE SPINES LIE FLAT UNLESS THERE IS DANGER

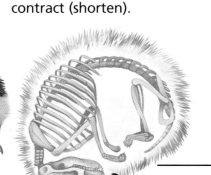

THE HEDGEHOG ROLLS INTO A BALL IF FRIGHTENED

AS THE SPINE MUSCLES CONTRACT, THE SPINES ARE RAISED

WHEN THE BODY IS DEFLATED, THE SPINES LIE FLAT

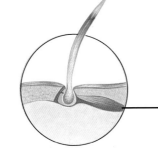

Colorful chameleons

Chameleons are gentle, slow moving lizards that can change color to match their surroundings. They also change color depending on their mood. When a chameleon becomes angry a brown substance in its skin, called melanin, is pushed to the surface. This darkens its color. Other colors are produced by special red, yellow, blue, and white cells in its skin. When a chameleon is calm its skin changes to green. Green is produced when its yellow skin cells enlarge over its blue cells. The chameleon's color change is rapid and controlled by the brain and chemicals in the blood.

THE SKIN IS MADE UP OF MILLIONS OF CELLS

A CHAMELEON'S EYES STICK OUT AND GIVE ALL-ROUND VISION

A MUSCULAR TONGUE DARTS OUT OF ITS MOUTH TO CATCH AN INSECT, A STICKY TIP WILL CATCH THE FLY

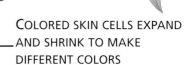

FINGERS AND TOES GIVE A FIRM GRIP

COLORED SKIN CELLS EXPAND AND SHRINK TO MAKE DIFFERENT COLORS

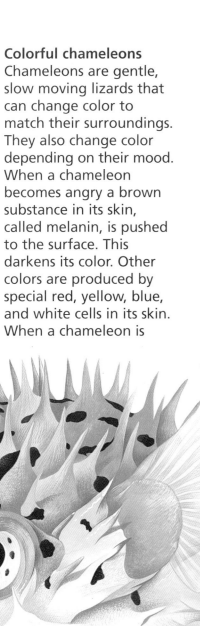

Porcupine fish

Porcupine fish are not designed to swim fast. Instead, they are designed to survive well. They have an armor of spines to protect them. If necessary they can inflate their bodies by swallowing water or air, and swell like a balloon. Once inflated they float, often upside down. As a floating ball of spines it is almost impossible for a predator to bite them, let alone swallow them!

THE NORMALLY SMALL PORCUPINE FISH GROWS INTO A THREATENING BALL OF SPINES

Tortoise shell

Tortoises and their cousins, turtles and terrapins, live inside a tough, protective shell. When they are in danger they can hide their legs, head, and tail inside the shell. The shell is made of bony plates that fit together like a jigsaw puzzle. A tough horny layer covers and protects the whole shell. The tortoise's body is fixed to the shell along its backbone, and at its hips and shoulders.

THE TORTOISE'S LEGS, TAIL, AND HEAD ARE TUCKED INSIDE THE SHELL

THE PORCUPINE FISH'S WIDTH INCREASES FROM 2 TO 8 INCHES

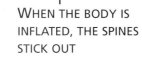
WHEN THE BODY IS INFLATED, THE SPINES STICK OUT

Inside Shells

SOME ANIMALS live inside a shell. They belong to the mollusk family, which includes snails, clams, and mussels. Octopus and squid are also mollusks but they do not have a shell. Mollusks live in water – in the sea, and in rivers, lakes, and ponds – and on land. Their body is made up of four parts. There is a head, with eyes, tentacles, and a mouth. There is also a muscular foot. Above the foot is a lump which holds the internal organs. Finally, there is a sheet of tissue, called the mantle, which grows over the lump and produces the shell. Some mollusks have more than one shell. These are made of a tough chalky substance. Between the body tissues and the mantle is a space which holds the gills (for breathing) and openings from the intestine, reproductive organs, and kidneys.

Snail

Snails glide along on a large foot. This does not simply help the snail to get from place to place; it is also joined with the head and contains many of its organs, including its brain, eyes, tentacles, and mouth. This is why snails are called gastropods, which means 'head-foot'. Their long coiled intestine is tucked away inside their shell, together with the kidney and reproductive organs. Snails mostly eat plant material but some eat other snails, drilling holes into them to get at them.

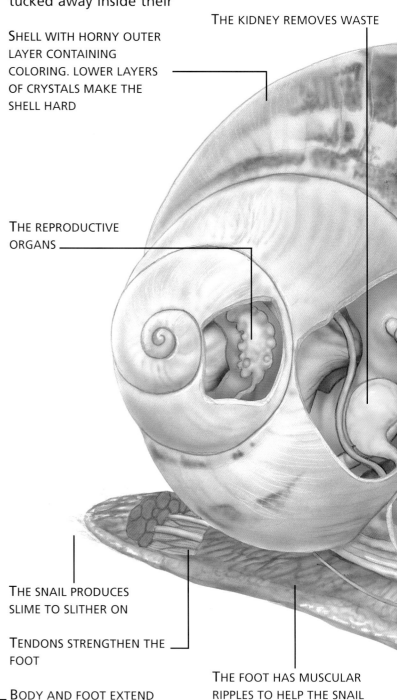

THE KIDNEY REMOVES WASTE

SHELL WITH HORNY OUTER LAYER CONTAINING COLORING. LOWER LAYERS OF CRYSTALS MAKE THE SHELL HARD

THE REPRODUCTIVE ORGANS

THE SNAIL PRODUCES SLIME TO SLITHER ON

TENDONS STRENGTHEN THE FOOT

BODY AND FOOT EXTEND THROUGH THE APERTURE

THE FOOT HAS MUSCULAR RIPPLES TO HELP THE SNAIL GLIDE ALONG

Spiral shell

Over 75,000 different kinds of snails are known. Each snail lives in its own type of colored shell. The shell has an opening called the aperture and is usually twisted into a spiral. Each spiral twist is called a whorl. Shells are colored for camouflage or to warn off predators because they are poisonous. The largest, the trumpet conch, can reach over 14 feet while the smallest, the pupa, is less than 16 inches long.

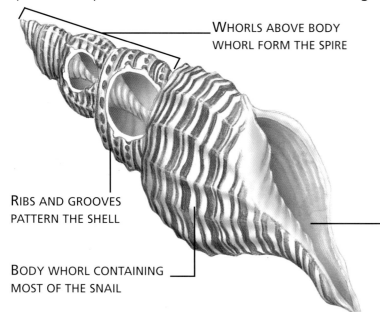

WHORLS ABOVE BODY WHORL FORM THE SPIRE

RIBS AND GROOVES PATTERN THE SHELL

BODY WHORL CONTAINING MOST OF THE SNAIL

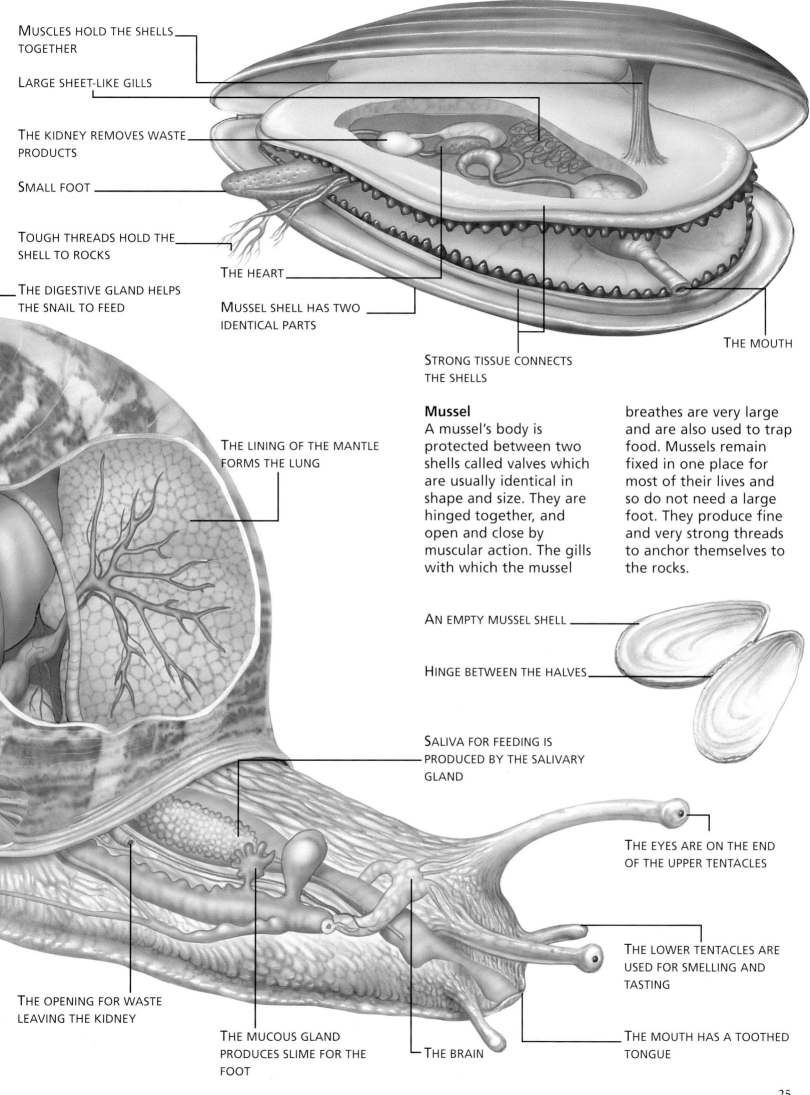

MUSCLES HOLD THE SHELLS TOGETHER

LARGE SHEET-LIKE GILLS

THE KIDNEY REMOVES WASTE PRODUCTS

SMALL FOOT

TOUGH THREADS HOLD THE SHELL TO ROCKS

THE DIGESTIVE GLAND HELPS THE SNAIL TO FEED

THE HEART

MUSSEL SHELL HAS TWO IDENTICAL PARTS

STRONG TISSUE CONNECTS THE SHELLS

THE MOUTH

THE LINING OF THE MANTLE FORMS THE LUNG

Mussel

A mussel's body is protected between two shells called valves which are usually identical in shape and size. They are hinged together, and open and close by muscular action. The gills with which the mussel breathes are very large and are also used to trap food. Mussels remain fixed in one place for most of their lives and so do not need a large foot. They produce fine and very strong threads to anchor themselves to the rocks.

AN EMPTY MUSSEL SHELL

HINGE BETWEEN THE HALVES

SALIVA FOR FEEDING IS PRODUCED BY THE SALIVARY GLAND

THE EYES ARE ON THE END OF THE UPPER TENTACLES

THE LOWER TENTACLES ARE USED FOR SMELLING AND TASTING

THE OPENING FOR WASTE LEAVING THE KIDNEY

THE MUCOUS GLAND PRODUCES SLIME FOR THE FOOT

THE BRAIN

THE MOUTH HAS A TOOTHED TONGUE

Spineless Life

MANY ANIMALS do not have a backbone. They are called invertebrates and include corals, worms, insects, and snails. Their muscles are supported by firm tissue, bags of gas or liquid, or a hard outer skeleton. Animals with no hard skeleton make a soft, easy meal, so some hide away in tubes or burrows; others are able to defend themselves with spines and stings.

The Portuguese man-of-war is a soft-bodied invertebrate. It is unusual in that it is made up of various small animals called polyps. Each polyp performs a different function: feeding, digesting, stinging, reproducing, and keeping afloat. It is blown along on the warm seas, kept afloat by a bladder full of gas, which acts as a sail. Its tentacles hang down several feet catching fish to eat.

THE GAS-FILLED BLADDER ACTS AS A SAIL

A WEB OF NERVE CELLS CARRIES INFORMATION TO THE DIFFERENT ANIMALS IN THE COLONY

POLYPS HAVE DIFFERENT FUNCTIONS, INCLUDING FEEDING, DIGESTION, AND REPRODUCTION

THE FEEDING POLYPS' TENTACLES CONTRACT (SHORTEN), PULLING PREY UP TO BE DIGESTED

DOZENS OF TENTACLES, HANGING DOWN 33 FEET, ARE USED TO SNARE PASSING PREY

Deadly weapons

The tentacles on a man-of-war carry special cells called cnidocysts that contain deadly weapons. When touched, triggers fire poison-filled threads. The threads shoot out and spear the victim, injecting it with poison. Once fired the cells are replaced by new ones.

A BARB (LIKE A FISH-HOOK) IS RELEASED WITH THE POISON-FILLED THREAD

EACH POISONOUS CELL HAS A TRIGGER

CELLS THAT HAVE BEEN FIRED ARE REPLACED

THE PREY IS STUNNED BY THE POISONOUS STING, SNARED BY THE THREADS, AND PULLED UP BY THE TENTACLES

26

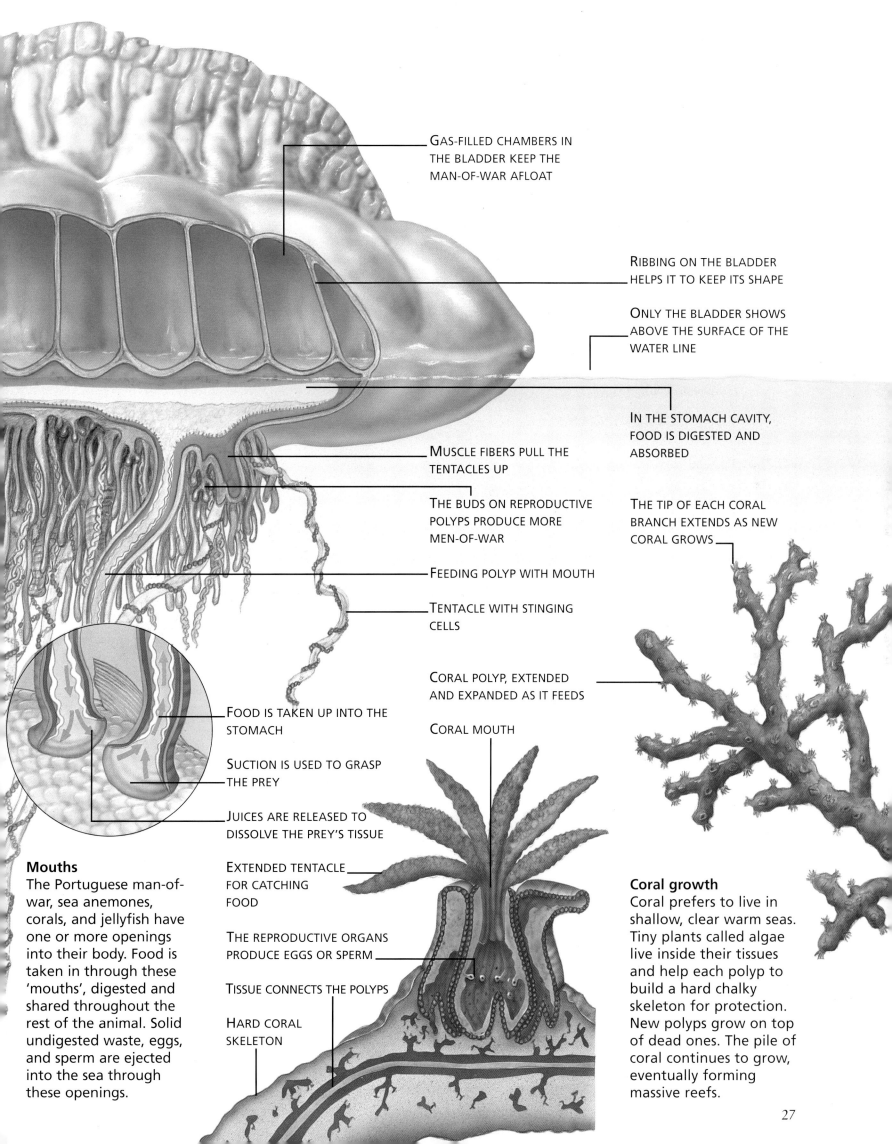

GAS-FILLED CHAMBERS IN THE BLADDER KEEP THE MAN-OF-WAR AFLOAT

RIBBING ON THE BLADDER HELPS IT TO KEEP ITS SHAPE

ONLY THE BLADDER SHOWS ABOVE THE SURFACE OF THE WATER LINE

IN THE STOMACH CAVITY, FOOD IS DIGESTED AND ABSORBED

MUSCLE FIBERS PULL THE TENTACLES UP

THE BUDS ON REPRODUCTIVE POLYPS PRODUCE MORE MEN-OF-WAR

THE TIP OF EACH CORAL BRANCH EXTENDS AS NEW CORAL GROWS

FEEDING POLYP WITH MOUTH

TENTACLE WITH STINGING CELLS

CORAL POLYP, EXTENDED AND EXPANDED AS IT FEEDS

CORAL MOUTH

FOOD IS TAKEN UP INTO THE STOMACH

SUCTION IS USED TO GRASP THE PREY

JUICES ARE RELEASED TO DISSOLVE THE PREY'S TISSUE

EXTENDED TENTACLE FOR CATCHING FOOD

THE REPRODUCTIVE ORGANS PRODUCE EGGS OR SPERM

TISSUE CONNECTS THE POLYPS

HARD CORAL SKELETON

Mouths

The Portuguese man-of-war, sea anemones, corals, and jellyfish have one or more openings into their body. Food is taken in through these 'mouths', digested and shared throughout the rest of the animal. Solid undigested waste, eggs, and sperm are ejected into the sea through these openings.

Coral growth

Coral prefers to live in shallow, clear warm seas. Tiny plants called algae live inside their tissues and help each polyp to build a hard chalky skeleton for protection. New polyps grow on top of dead ones. The pile of coral continues to grow, eventually forming massive reefs.

Insect Life

THERE ARE more insects and different types of insects than any other animal. Insects make use of almost every type of environment, from the dark, damp forest floor to the dry heat of the desert. Their bodies are covered in a tough but light armor called cuticle. Cuticle can be soft and flexible or very hard. For example, the jaw of a cockroach can cut through a lead pipe! Cuticle is also waterproof. The cuticle is one of the main reasons that insects are so successful.

The insect's body is divided into three parts: head, thorax, and abdomen. The head carries the eyes, antennae (feelers), and mouth parts, and it also houses the brain. The thorax supports the wings and three pairs of legs, and is the powerhouse for the insect's movement. The abdomen holds the intestines and other internal organs.

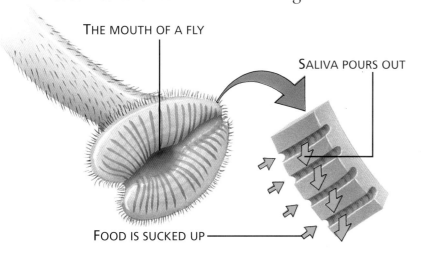

THE MOUTH OF A FLY

SALIVA POURS OUT

FOOD IS SUCKED UP

Tools for eating
Insects have three sets of 'jaws', or mouth parts. The designs of these parts can vary enormously between different species. Some chew, others bite or cut, stab, pierce, rasp, pinch, drill, inject, or lick.

Flies eat almost any liquid or semi-liquid food, from rotting filth to nectar. Saliva is poured down from the fly's salivary glands and spread onto the food. The saliva mixes with the food and is used to soften it if it is very hard. The fly then uses delicate tubes to suck the meal up into its stomach.

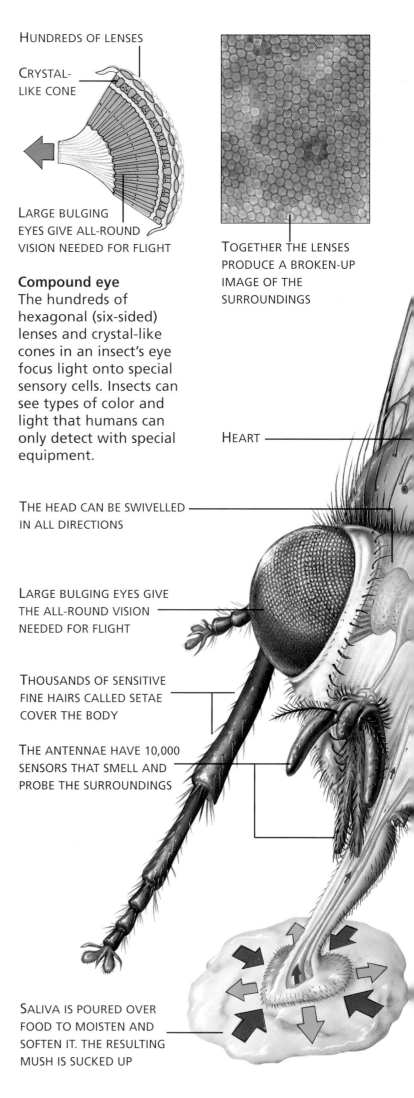

HUNDREDS OF LENSES

CRYSTAL-LIKE CONE

LARGE BULGING EYES GIVE ALL-ROUND VISION NEEDED FOR FLIGHT

TOGETHER THE LENSES PRODUCE A BROKEN-UP IMAGE OF THE SURROUNDINGS

Compound eye
The hundreds of hexagonal (six-sided) lenses and crystal-like cones in an insect's eye focus light onto special sensory cells. Insects can see types of color and light that humans can only detect with special equipment.

HEART

THE HEAD CAN BE SWIVELLED IN ALL DIRECTIONS

LARGE BULGING EYES GIVE THE ALL-ROUND VISION NEEDED FOR FLIGHT

THOUSANDS OF SENSITIVE FINE HAIRS CALLED SETAE COVER THE BODY

THE ANTENNAE HAVE 10,000 SENSORS THAT SMELL AND PROBE THE SURROUNDINGS

SALIVA IS POURED OVER FOOD TO MOISTEN AND SOFTEN IT. THE RESULTING MUSH IS SUCKED UP

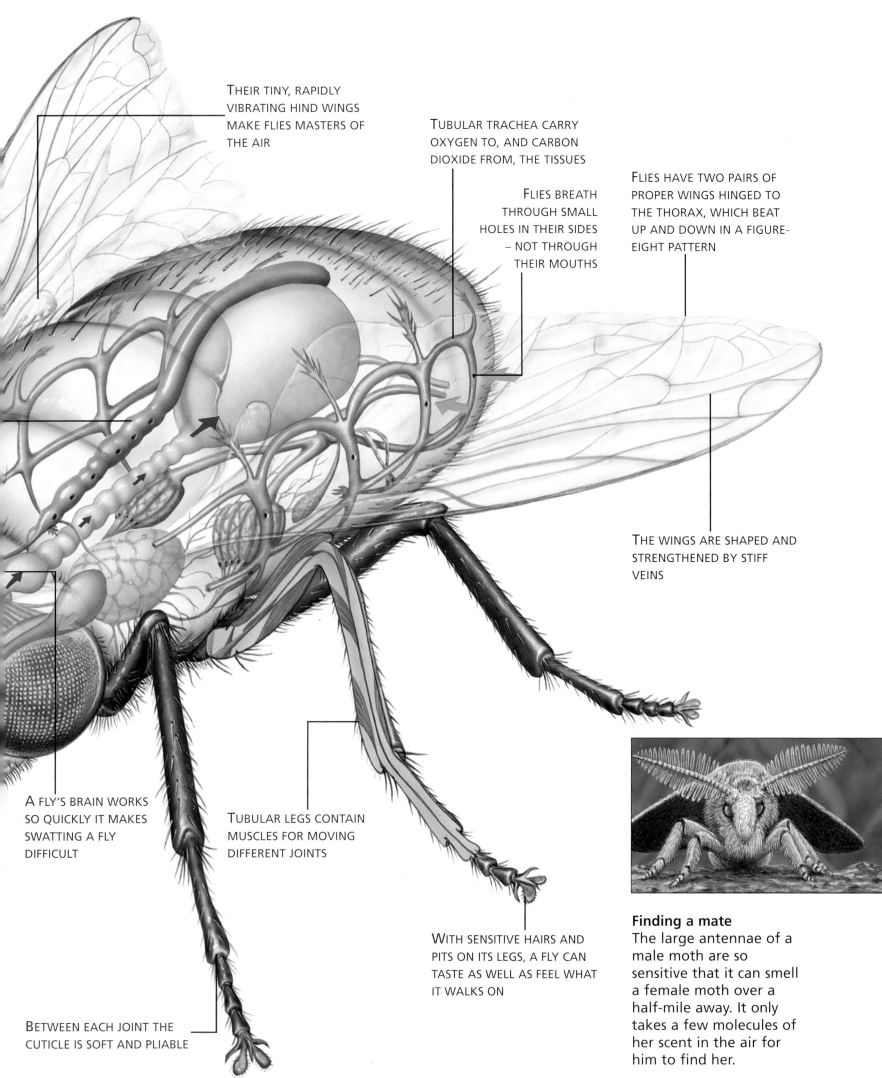

THEIR TINY, RAPIDLY VIBRATING HIND WINGS MAKE FLIES MASTERS OF THE AIR

TUBULAR TRACHEA CARRY OXYGEN TO, AND CARBON DIOXIDE FROM, THE TISSUES

FLIES BREATH THROUGH SMALL HOLES IN THEIR SIDES – NOT THROUGH THEIR MOUTHS

FLIES HAVE TWO PAIRS OF PROPER WINGS HINGED TO THE THORAX, WHICH BEAT UP AND DOWN IN A FIGURE-EIGHT PATTERN

THE WINGS ARE SHAPED AND STRENGTHENED BY STIFF VEINS

A FLY'S BRAIN WORKS SO QUICKLY IT MAKES SWATTING A FLY DIFFICULT

TUBULAR LEGS CONTAIN MUSCLES FOR MOVING DIFFERENT JOINTS

WITH SENSITIVE HAIRS AND PITS ON ITS LEGS, A FLY CAN TASTE AS WELL AS FEEL WHAT IT WALKS ON

BETWEEN EACH JOINT THE CUTICLE IS SOFT AND PLIABLE

Finding a mate
The large antennae of a male moth are so sensitive that it can smell a female moth over a half-mile away. It only takes a few molecules of her scent in the air for him to find her.

Changing Shape

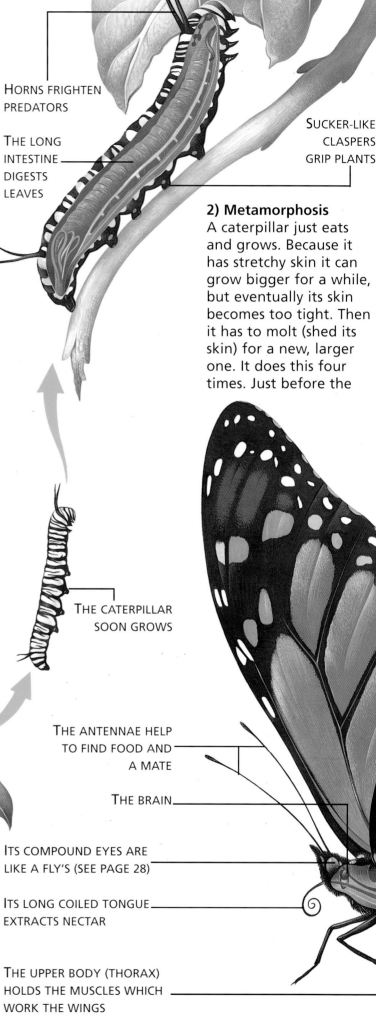

HORNS FRIGHTEN PREDATORS

THE LONG INTESTINE DIGESTS LEAVES

SUCKER-LIKE CLASPERS GRIP PLANTS

MONARCH BUTTERFLIES live in North America. Like all butterflies, they begin life as caterpillars. While they are caterpillars, monarchs eat the leaves of milkweed plants for energy and growth. Other animals find these plants poisonous and leave them alone, but these caterpillars are not affected by the poison. In fact, they make use of it for their own defense. They store it, making themselves taste nasty so predators (hunters) leave them alone, even after they have become butterflies.

After metamorphosis (the process of changing shape), the caterpillars become butterflies. Like all butterflies, the monarch butterfly sips nectar from flowers. Nectar provides the energy needed to fly. They fly to new places so they can find plants to lay their eggs on. They also use flight to escape from enemies or find a mate.

2) Metamorphosis
A caterpillar just eats and grows. Because it has stretchy skin it can grow bigger for a while, but eventually its skin becomes too tight. Then it has to molt (shed its skin) for a new, larger one. It does this four times. Just before the

THE CATERPILLAR SOON GROWS

A BABY CATERPILLAR CLIMBING FROM ITS EGG

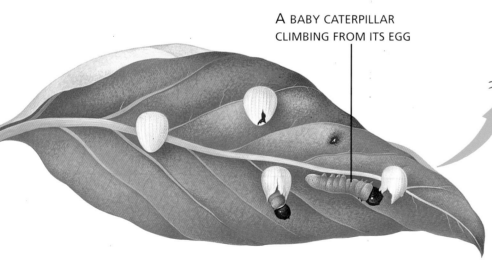

THE ANTENNAE HELP TO FIND FOOD AND A MATE

THE BRAIN

ITS COMPOUND EYES ARE LIKE A FLY'S (SEE PAGE 28)

ITS LONG COILED TONGUE EXTRACTS NECTAR

THE UPPER BODY (THORAX) HOLDS THE MUSCLES WHICH WORK THE WINGS

1) From egg to caterpillar
The female monarch butterfly lays her eggs in groups on the surface of a leaf. Some other butterflies lay them singly. The eggs are tiny but very tough. They protect the growing baby caterpillars inside from rain, sun, and parasites (insects that live on other insects). To escape from the eggs the baby caterpillars bite their way out using their tiny jaws. After hatching, the caterpillars eat the rest of the egg shells before moving away to feed on leaves.

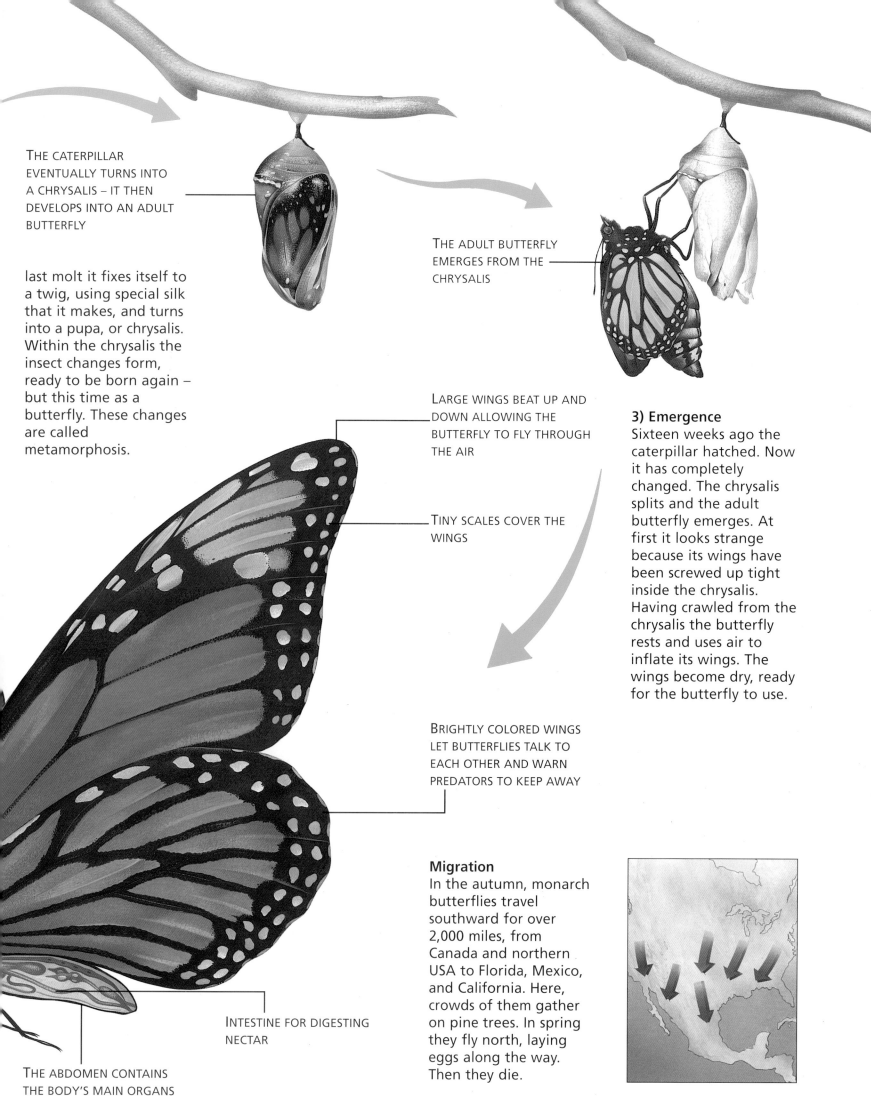

THE CATERPILLAR EVENTUALLY TURNS INTO A CHRYSALIS – IT THEN DEVELOPS INTO AN ADULT BUTTERFLY

last molt it fixes itself to a twig, using special silk that it makes, and turns into a pupa, or chrysalis. Within the chrysalis the insect changes form, ready to be born again – but this time as a butterfly. These changes are called metamorphosis.

THE ADULT BUTTERFLY EMERGES FROM THE CHRYSALIS

LARGE WINGS BEAT UP AND DOWN ALLOWING THE BUTTERFLY TO FLY THROUGH THE AIR

TINY SCALES COVER THE WINGS

BRIGHTLY COLORED WINGS LET BUTTERFLIES TALK TO EACH OTHER AND WARN PREDATORS TO KEEP AWAY

INTESTINE FOR DIGESTING NECTAR

THE ABDOMEN CONTAINS THE BODY'S MAIN ORGANS

3) Emergence
Sixteen weeks ago the caterpillar hatched. Now it has completely changed. The chrysalis splits and the adult butterfly emerges. At first it looks strange because its wings have been screwed up tight inside the chrysalis. Having crawled from the chrysalis the butterfly rests and uses air to inflate its wings. The wings become dry, ready for the butterfly to use.

Migration
In the autumn, monarch butterflies travel southward for over 2,000 miles, from Canada and northern USA to Florida, Mexico, and California. Here, crowds of them gather on pine trees. In spring they fly north, laying eggs along the way. Then they die.

A Frog's Life

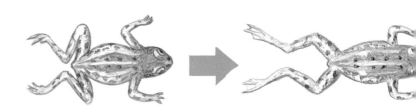

LIKE ALL FROGS, the Colombian horned frog is cold-blooded and has a moist skin. Horned frogs like this one live in tropical American forests, hiding among the moss and dead leaves of the forest floor. They are very aggressive and will even try to eat animals that are bigger than they are.

Frogs have a large head, bulging eyes, and a wide mouth. The front legs are shorter than the back legs, which usually have an extra long heel for jumping. Frogs can swim, and they depend on water to keep themselves moist and to raise their young. They can breathe both in and out of water. When underwater they breathe through their skin.

Swimming
While bringing the front legs forward, the back legs are drawn upwards towards the body. Then the front legs swing to the sides and the back legs shoot backwards, thrusting the frog forwards.

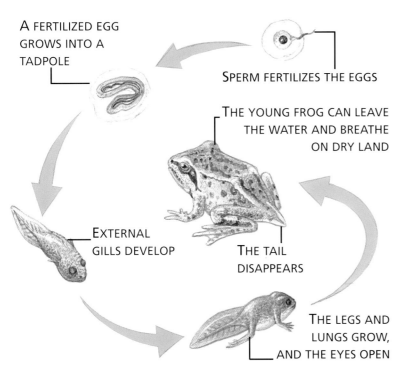

A FERTILIZED EGG GROWS INTO A TADPOLE

SPERM FERTILIZES THE EGGS

THE YOUNG FROG CAN LEAVE THE WATER AND BREATHE ON DRY LAND

EXTERNAL GILLS DEVELOP

THE TAIL DISAPPEARS

THE LEGS AND LUNGS GROW, AND THE EYES OPEN

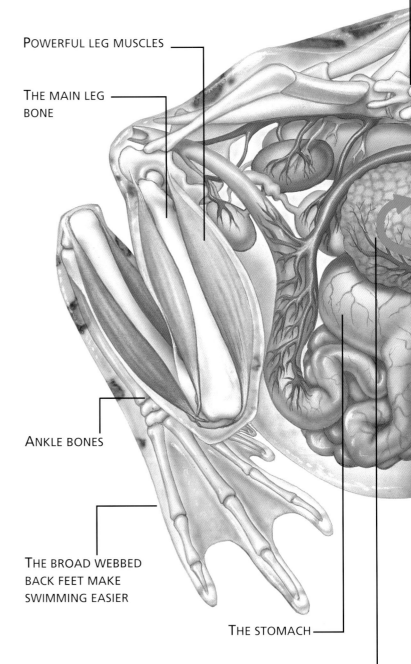

THE SPINAL COLUMN (BACKBONE) IS MADE UP OF SMALL BONES CALLED VERTEBRAE

POWERFUL LEG MUSCLES

THE MAIN LEG BONE

ANKLE BONES

THE BROAD WEBBED BACK FEET MAKE SWIMMING EASIER

THE STOMACH

ON LAND AIR IS BREATHED IN AND OUT OF THE LUNGS

Tadpole to frog
A female frog lays her eggs in water. The mass of eggs is called spawn. The spawn is fertilized by sperm from the male frog. The fertilized eggs then grow into balls of cells which develop into tadpoles. At first, tadpoles are blind and breathe underwater using external gills. But gradually they change into frogs – a process called metamorphosis. Their eyes open, their legs grow, and their lungs develop. When their lungs have grown they can leave the water and use the lungs to breathe.

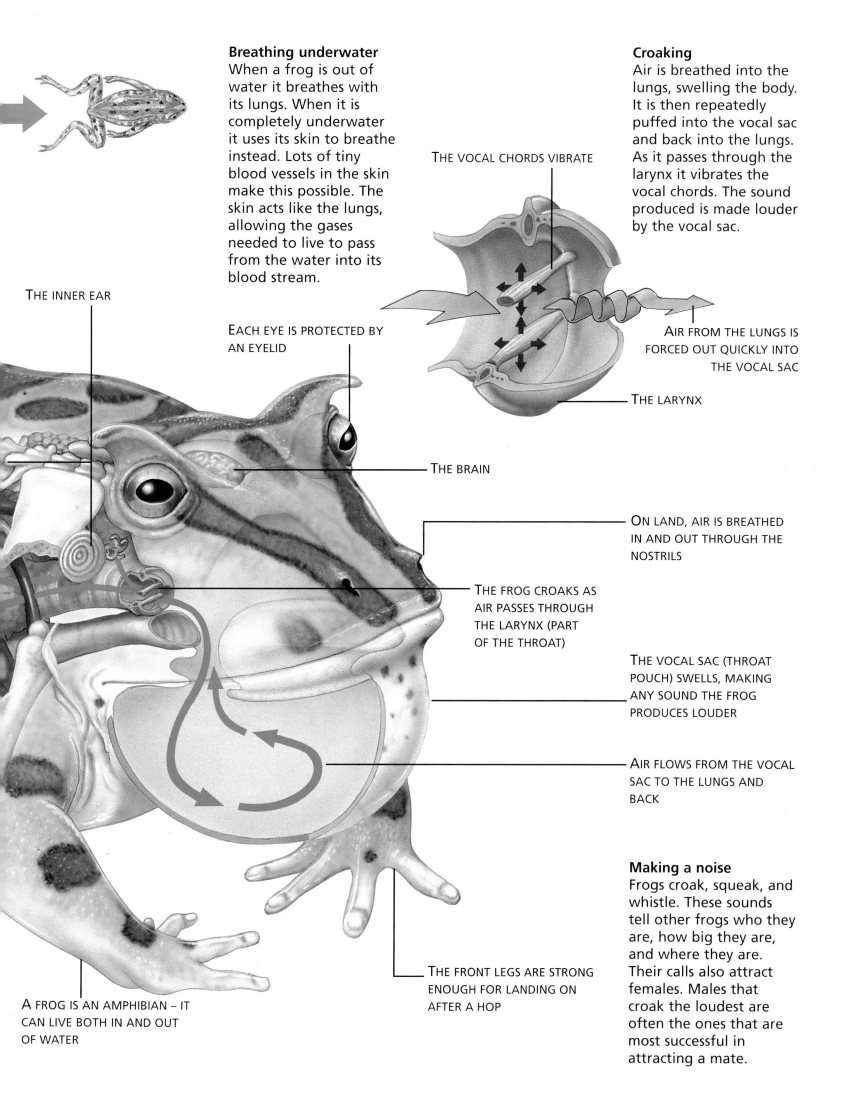

Breathing underwater
When a frog is out of water it breathes with its lungs. When it is completely underwater it uses its skin to breathe instead. Lots of tiny blood vessels in the skin make this possible. The skin acts like the lungs, allowing the gases needed to live to pass from the water into its blood stream.

Croaking
Air is breathed into the lungs, swelling the body. It is then repeatedly puffed into the vocal sac and back into the lungs. As it passes through the larynx it vibrates the vocal chords. The sound produced is made louder by the vocal sac.

THE VOCAL CHORDS VIBRATE

AIR FROM THE LUNGS IS FORCED OUT QUICKLY INTO THE VOCAL SAC

THE LARYNX

THE INNER EAR

EACH EYE IS PROTECTED BY AN EYELID

THE BRAIN

ON LAND, AIR IS BREATHED IN AND OUT THROUGH THE NOSTRILS

THE FROG CROAKS AS AIR PASSES THROUGH THE LARYNX (PART OF THE THROAT)

THE VOCAL SAC (THROAT POUCH) SWELLS, MAKING ANY SOUND THE FROG PRODUCES LOUDER

AIR FLOWS FROM THE VOCAL SAC TO THE LUNGS AND BACK

Making a noise
Frogs croak, squeak, and whistle. These sounds tell other frogs who they are, how big they are, and where they are. Their calls also attract females. Males that croak the loudest are often the ones that are most successful in attracting a mate.

THE FRONT LEGS ARE STRONG ENOUGH FOR LANDING ON AFTER A HOP

A FROG IS AN AMPHIBIAN – IT CAN LIVE BOTH IN AND OUT OF WATER

Baby Mammals

MAMMALS ARE warm-blooded animals which feed their young with milk. Most mammals are covered in hair, which helps to keep them warm. Their milk comes from special milk glands called mammary glands. Even mammals that lay eggs, like the spiny anteater and duck-billed platypus, produce milk for their young. All other mammals give birth to live babies, which develop inside the mother's uterus. They are attached to the uterus by a tube called the umbilical cord. Through the cord they get food and oxygen, which helps them grow. Small mammals develop faster than large ones: a mouse takes about 2 weeks to develop while an elephant takes 22 months. Humans develop for 9 months. When the mammal is ready to give birth, chemicals in her body cause her uterus to push the baby out.

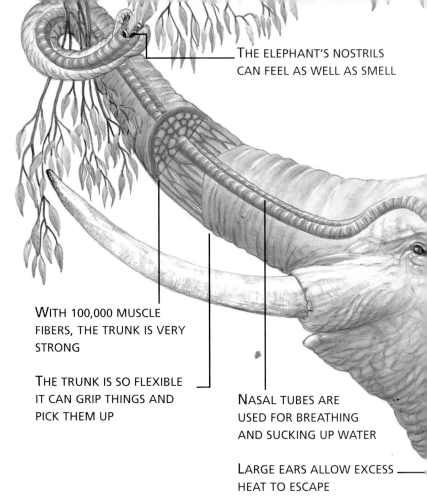

THE ELEPHANT'S NOSTRILS CAN FEEL AS WELL AS SMELL

WITH 100,000 MUSCLE FIBERS, THE TRUNK IS VERY STRONG

THE TRUNK IS SO FLEXIBLE IT CAN GRIP THINGS AND PICK THEM UP

NASAL TUBES ARE USED FOR BREATHING AND SUCKING UP WATER

LARGE EARS ALLOW EXCESS HEAT TO ESCAPE

Marsupials

Marsupials are mammals that give birth to babies which are not fully developed. The baby continues to develop in a pouch on the mother's tummy. In the pouch the baby can crawl to one of the mother's nipples to suck milk.

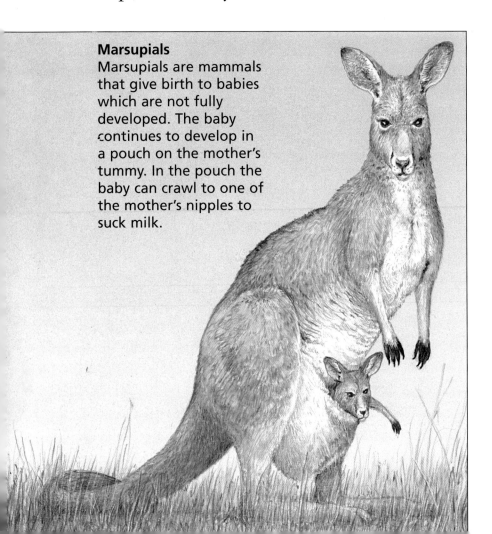

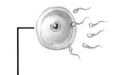

FERTILIZATION: A MALE SPERM-CELL JOINS AN EGG

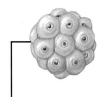

A BALL OF CELLS FORMS AT THREE DAYS

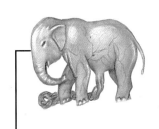

A TWO-MONTH OLD FOETUS (ACTUAL SIZE); ITS EYES ARE NOT YET FULLY DEVELOPED

Fertilization and development

Every mammal starts out as a tiny egg produced by the mother. To become a baby mammal the egg has to be joined by a sperm-cell from the father. This process is called fertilization. The fertilized cell divides into a ball of cells, which becomes fixed to the wall of the female's uterus. The ball of cells then develops into what we call a fetus, as its head, body, and legs begin to grow.

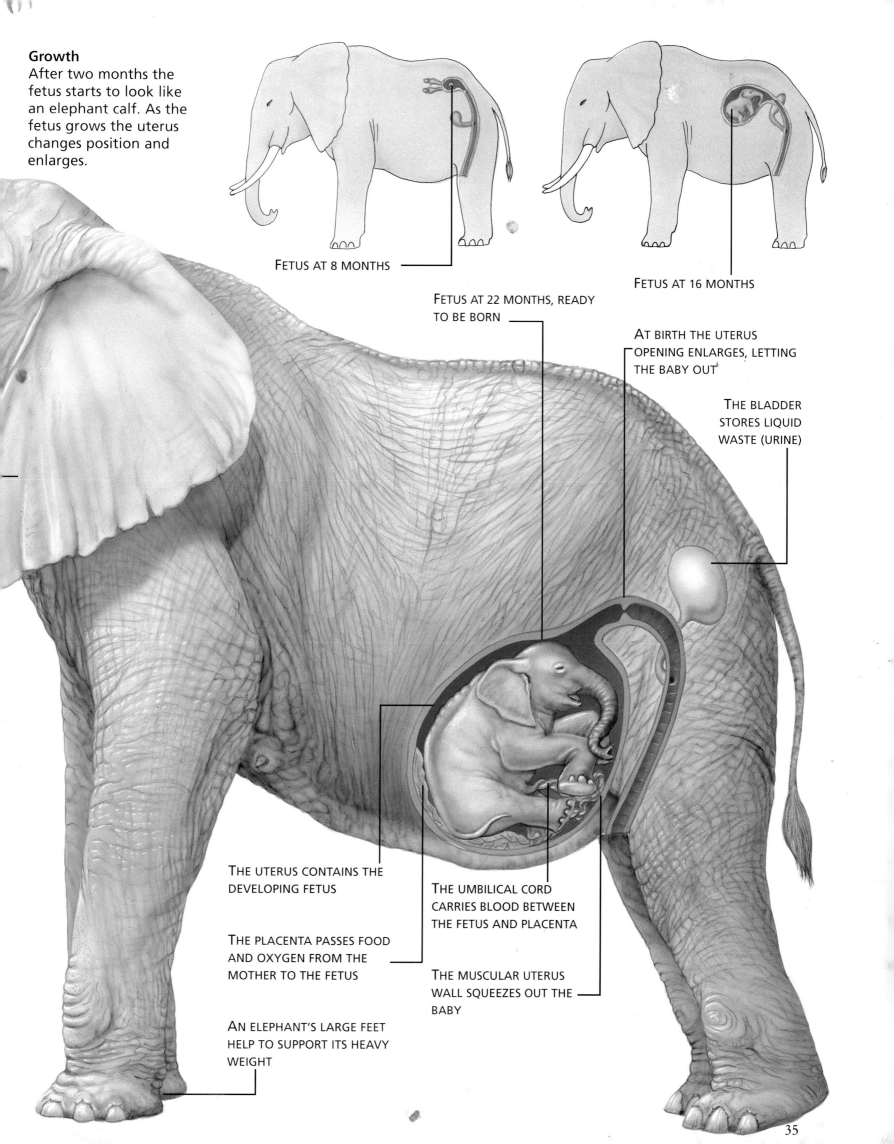

Growth
After two months the fetus starts to look like an elephant calf. As the fetus grows the uterus changes position and enlarges.

FETUS AT 8 MONTHS

FETUS AT 16 MONTHS

FETUS AT 22 MONTHS, READY TO BE BORN

AT BIRTH THE UTERUS OPENING ENLARGES, LETTING THE BABY OUT

THE BLADDER STORES LIQUID WASTE (URINE)

THE UTERUS CONTAINS THE DEVELOPING FETUS

THE UMBILICAL CORD CARRIES BLOOD BETWEEN THE FETUS AND PLACENTA

THE PLACENTA PASSES FOOD AND OXYGEN FROM THE MOTHER TO THE FETUS

THE MUSCULAR UTERUS WALL SQUEEZES OUT THE BABY

AN ELEPHANT'S LARGE FEET HELP TO SUPPORT ITS HEAVY WEIGHT

35

Hatching Eggs

PHEASANTS, LIKE ALL birds, lay eggs. Pheasants lay 8 to 15 eggs at a time. Eggs are strong rounded structures which hold and protect the chick as it develops. The shell is made of chalky crystals, which makes it strong, and it is lined with a tough membrane. This protects the chick from drying up and allows oxygen to pass in and carbon dioxide waste to travel out. Within the shell the chick rests in a soft jelly-like fluid. It receives food from the yellow bag of yolk. On the outside, egg shells are lightly colored and are often flecked with brown so that they are not easily seen within the nest. Nests help the hen to protect her eggs and make it possible for her to sit on them, keeping them warm.

Pheasant nests
It is important to hide the nest and eggs from foxes and stoats. To do this a simple hollow is scraped in the ground under a hedge or a layer of plants. It is sometimes lined with a little surrounding plant material. The plain olive-brown or grey colored eggs can hardly be seen.

Embryo development
After the female and male bird have mated, the tiny fertilized egg cell divides into more and more cells to form a patch of cells, the embryo. As the embryo develops the cells continue to divide, eventually organizing themselves into tissues and organs. Some of the cells move and form folds which later develop into different structures. But not all of the cells become part of the chick. Some become blood vessels that take food from the yolk to the developing chick, others form a bag to hold waste as the chick grows.

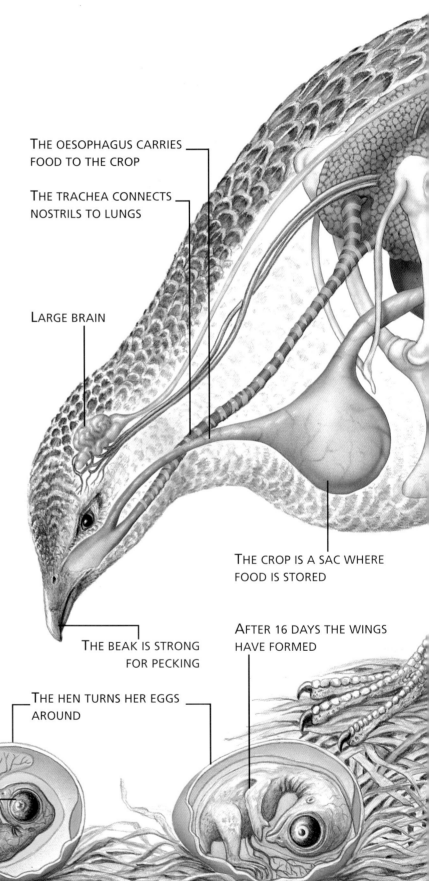

THE OESOPHAGUS CARRIES FOOD TO THE CROP

THE TRACHEA CONNECTS NOSTRILS TO LUNGS

LARGE BRAIN

THE CROP IS A SAC WHERE FOOD IS STORED

THE BEAK IS STRONG FOR PECKING

AFTER 16 DAYS THE WINGS HAVE FORMED

TWO DAYS AFTER THE EGG IS LAID, THE HEART IS PUMPING BLOOD TO THE YOLK-SAC

AFTER EIGHT DAYS THE MAIN ORGANS AND LARGE EYES HAVE DEVELOPED

THE HEN TURNS HER EGGS AROUND

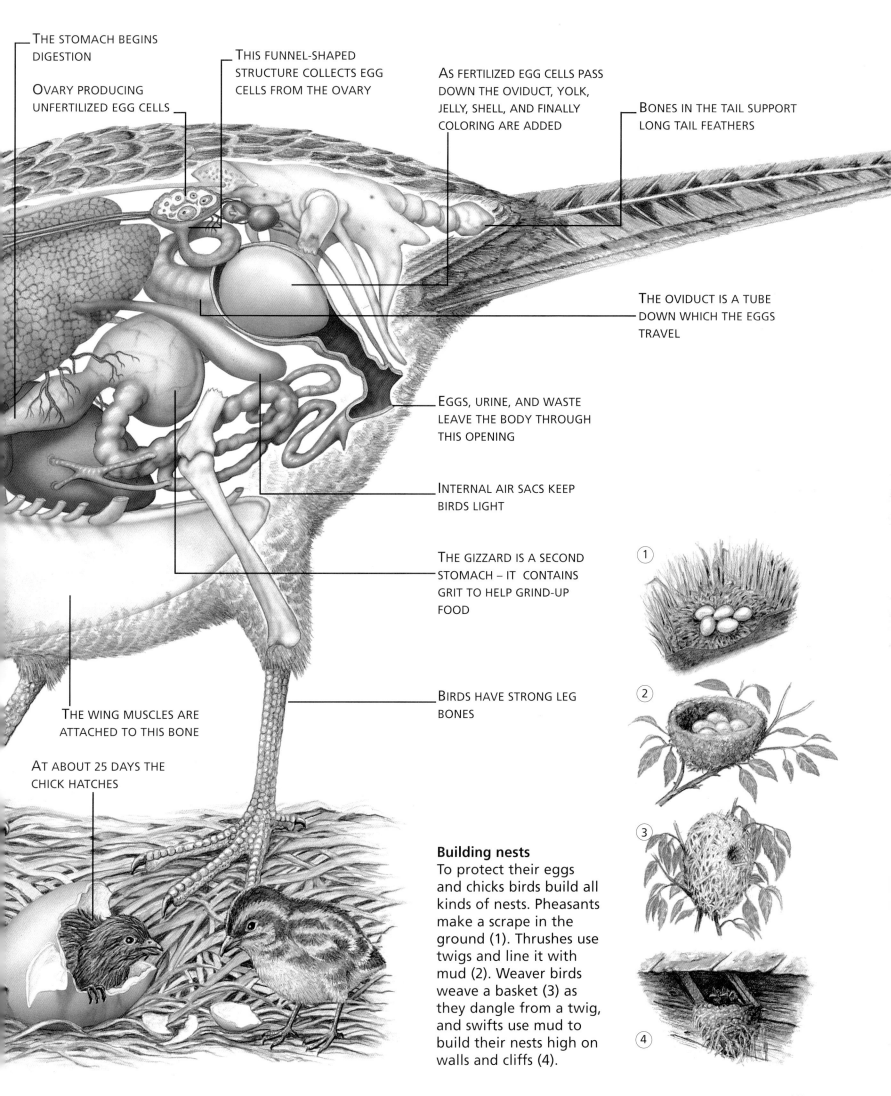

THE STOMACH BEGINS DIGESTION

OVARY PRODUCING UNFERTILIZED EGG CELLS

THIS FUNNEL-SHAPED STRUCTURE COLLECTS EGG CELLS FROM THE OVARY

AS FERTILIZED EGG CELLS PASS DOWN THE OVIDUCT, YOLK, JELLY, SHELL, AND FINALLY COLORING ARE ADDED

BONES IN THE TAIL SUPPORT LONG TAIL FEATHERS

THE OVIDUCT IS A TUBE DOWN WHICH THE EGGS TRAVEL

EGGS, URINE, AND WASTE LEAVE THE BODY THROUGH THIS OPENING

INTERNAL AIR SACS KEEP BIRDS LIGHT

THE GIZZARD IS A SECOND STOMACH – IT CONTAINS GRIT TO HELP GRIND-UP FOOD

BIRDS HAVE STRONG LEG BONES

THE WING MUSCLES ARE ATTACHED TO THIS BONE

AT ABOUT 25 DAYS THE CHICK HATCHES

Building nests
To protect their eggs and chicks birds build all kinds of nests. Pheasants make a scrape in the ground (1). Thrushes use twigs and line it with mud (2). Weaver birds weave a basket (3) as they dangle from a twig, and swifts use mud to build their nests high on walls and cliffs (4).

37

Desert Animals

CAMELS LIVE in deserts. Their bodies are specially designed to survive the desert's hot days and cold nights. They can also cope with the wind-blown sand and long periods without water. For nearly 4,000 years, since they were first domesticated (tamed) in Arabia, they have helped people live and travel in the desert. Camels can run at 10 mph – some are bred specially for racing. They can even swim. When walking, camels move at about 2 mph and can travel nearly 30 miles each day. But they do not like going up hills. Camels are able to carry loads of up to 2,000 pounds. This makes them ideal pack animals, which is why they are sometimes called 'ships of the desert'.

The camel's hump
Some camels have one hump, others have two. The one-humped dromedary originally lived in Arabia. The two-humped bactrian camel is found in Mongolia and Turkestan. A camel's hump is filled with fat. Well-fed camels have firm, upright humps. Once in the desert, away from a supply of food, they use the fat as a source of energy and water. When most of the fat has been used up the hump shrivels and flops over.

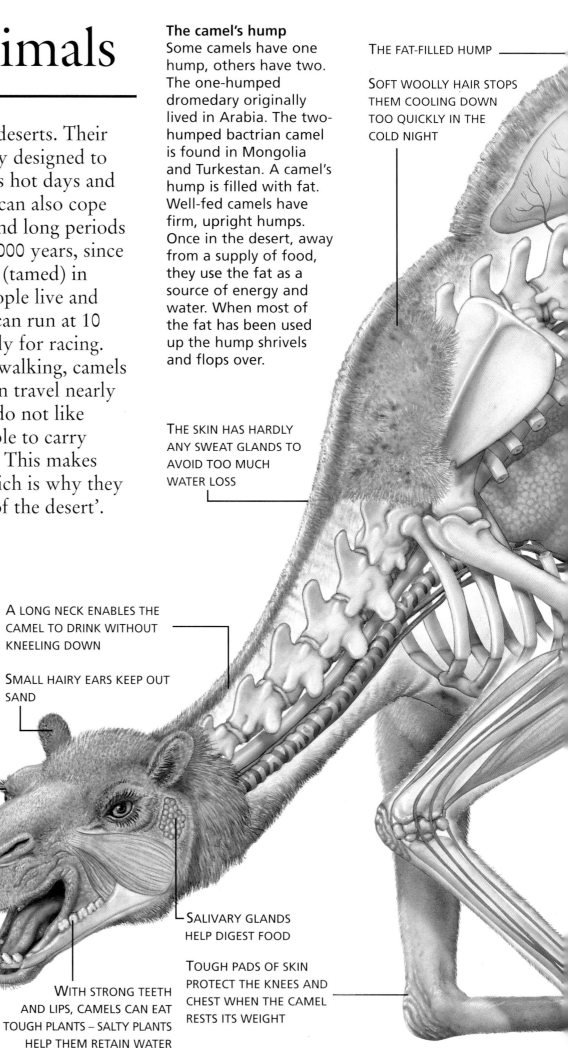

THE FAT-FILLED HUMP

SOFT WOOLLY HAIR STOPS THEM COOLING DOWN TOO QUICKLY IN THE COLD NIGHT

THE SKIN HAS HARDLY ANY SWEAT GLANDS TO AVOID TOO MUCH WATER LOSS

A LONG NECK ENABLES THE CAMEL TO DRINK WITHOUT KNEELING DOWN

SMALL HAIRY EARS KEEP OUT SAND

LONG EYELASHES AND BIG EYELIDS PROTECT THEIR EYES FROM THE SUN AND FLYING SAND

THEIR NOSTRILS CAN CLOSE TO KEEP OUT THE SAND

SALIVARY GLANDS HELP DIGEST FOOD

TOUGH PADS OF SKIN PROTECT THE KNEES AND CHEST WHEN THE CAMEL RESTS ITS WEIGHT

WITH STRONG TEETH AND LIPS, CAMELS CAN EAT TOUGH PLANTS – SALTY PLANTS HELP THEM RETAIN WATER

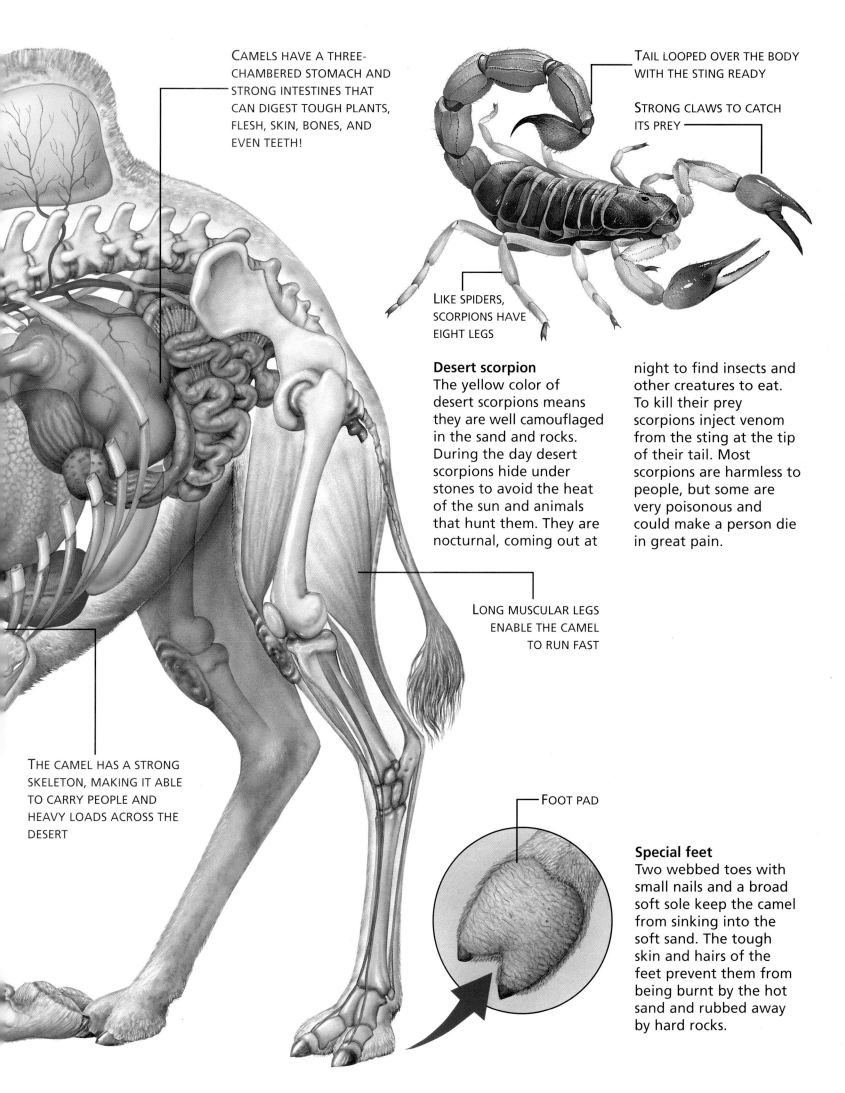

CAMELS HAVE A THREE-CHAMBERED STOMACH AND STRONG INTESTINES THAT CAN DIGEST TOUGH PLANTS, FLESH, SKIN, BONES, AND EVEN TEETH!

TAIL LOOPED OVER THE BODY WITH THE STING READY

STRONG CLAWS TO CATCH ITS PREY

LIKE SPIDERS, SCORPIONS HAVE EIGHT LEGS

Desert scorpion

The yellow color of desert scorpions means they are well camouflaged in the sand and rocks. During the day desert scorpions hide under stones to avoid the heat of the sun and animals that hunt them. They are nocturnal, coming out at night to find insects and other creatures to eat. To kill their prey scorpions inject venom from the sting at the tip of their tail. Most scorpions are harmless to people, but some are very poisonous and could make a person die in great pain.

LONG MUSCULAR LEGS ENABLE THE CAMEL TO RUN FAST

THE CAMEL HAS A STRONG SKELETON, MAKING IT ABLE TO CARRY PEOPLE AND HEAVY LOADS ACROSS THE DESERT

FOOT PAD

Special feet

Two webbed toes with small nails and a broad soft sole keep the camel from sinking into the soft sand. The tough skin and hairs of the feet prevent them from being burnt by the hot sand and rubbed away by hard rocks.

Arctic Animals

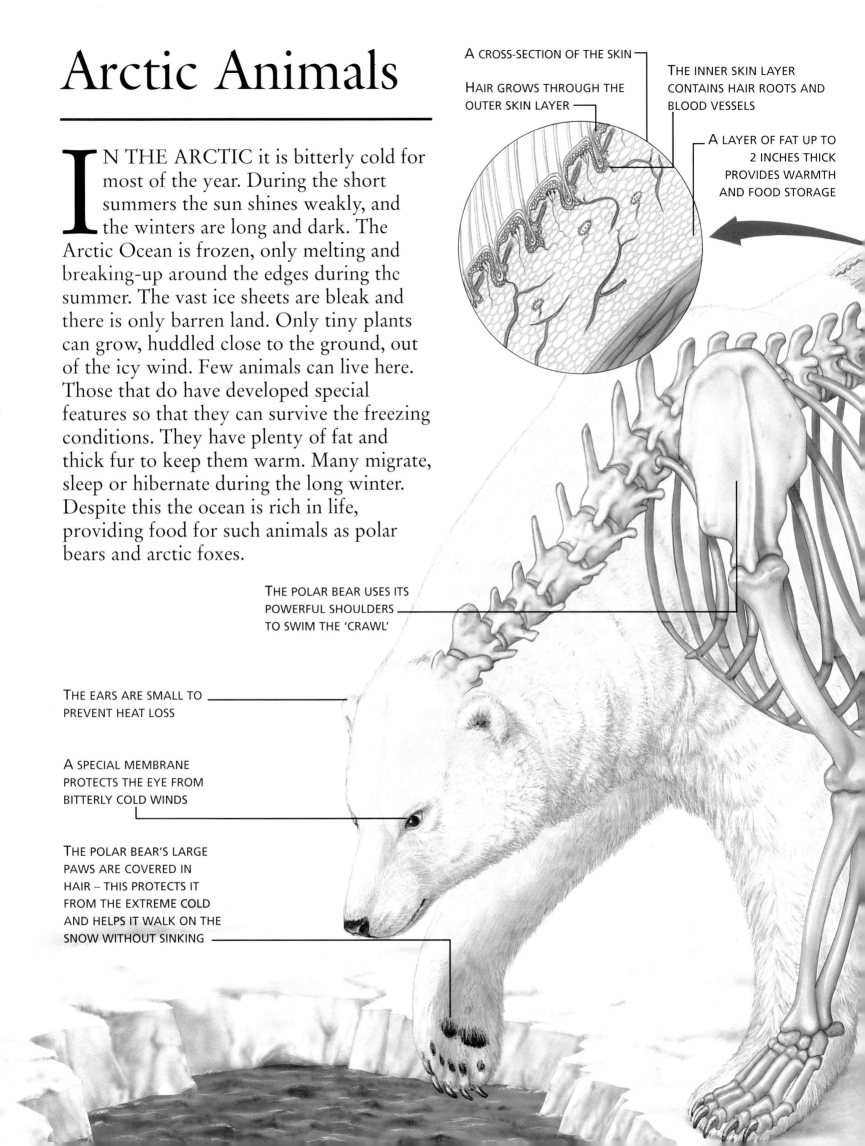

IN THE ARCTIC it is bitterly cold for most of the year. During the short summers the sun shines weakly, and the winters are long and dark. The Arctic Ocean is frozen, only melting and breaking-up around the edges during the summer. The vast ice sheets are bleak and there is only barren land. Only tiny plants can grow, huddled close to the ground, out of the icy wind. Few animals can live here. Those that do have developed special features so that they can survive the freezing conditions. They have plenty of fat and thick fur to keep them warm. Many migrate, sleep or hibernate during the long winter. Despite this the ocean is rich in life, providing food for such animals as polar bears and arctic foxes.

A CROSS-SECTION OF THE SKIN

HAIR GROWS THROUGH THE OUTER SKIN LAYER

THE INNER SKIN LAYER CONTAINS HAIR ROOTS AND BLOOD VESSELS

A LAYER OF FAT UP TO 2 INCHES THICK PROVIDES WARMTH AND FOOD STORAGE

THE POLAR BEAR USES ITS POWERFUL SHOULDERS TO SWIM THE 'CRAWL'

THE EARS ARE SMALL TO PREVENT HEAT LOSS

A SPECIAL MEMBRANE PROTECTS THE EYE FROM BITTERLY COLD WINDS

THE POLAR BEAR'S LARGE PAWS ARE COVERED IN HAIR – THIS PROTECTS IT FROM THE EXTREME COLD AND HELPS IT WALK ON THE SNOW WITHOUT SINKING

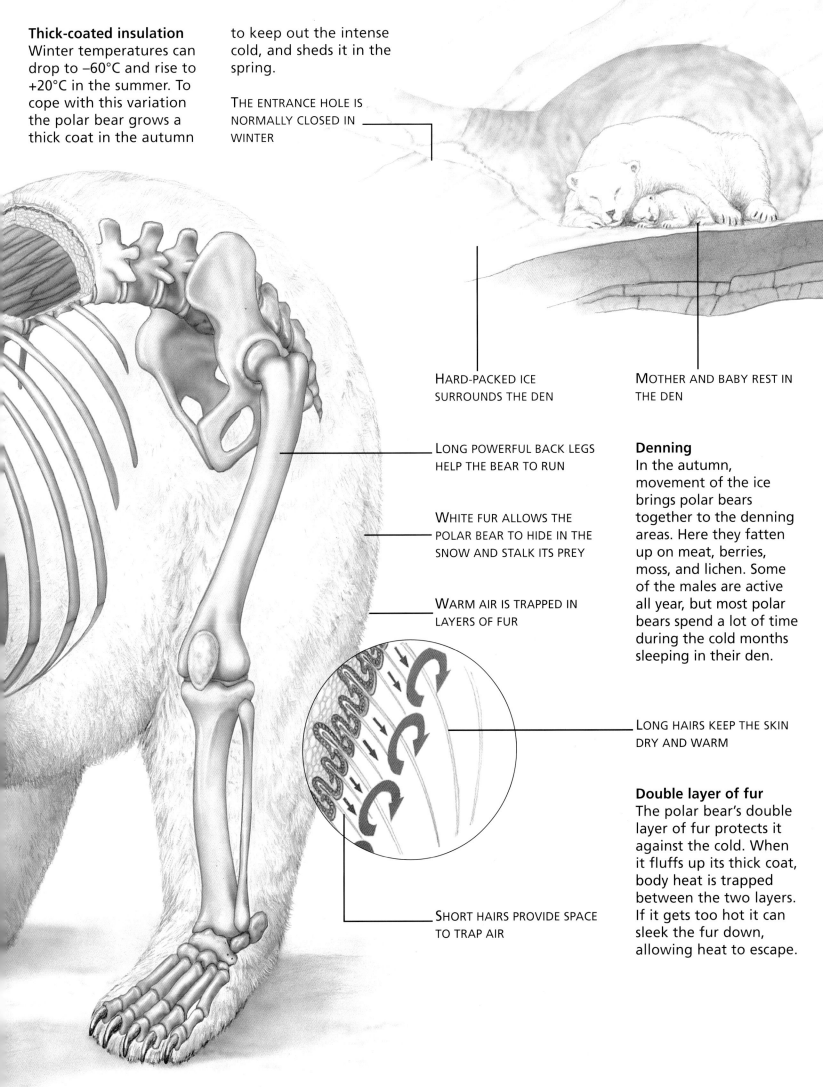

Thick-coated insulation
Winter temperatures can drop to –60°C and rise to +20°C in the summer. To cope with this variation the polar bear grows a thick coat in the autumn to keep out the intense cold, and sheds it in the spring.

THE ENTRANCE HOLE IS NORMALLY CLOSED IN WINTER

HARD-PACKED ICE SURROUNDS THE DEN

MOTHER AND BABY REST IN THE DEN

LONG POWERFUL BACK LEGS HELP THE BEAR TO RUN

WHITE FUR ALLOWS THE POLAR BEAR TO HIDE IN THE SNOW AND STALK ITS PREY

WARM AIR IS TRAPPED IN LAYERS OF FUR

Denning
In the autumn, movement of the ice brings polar bears together to the denning areas. Here they fatten up on meat, berries, moss, and lichen. Some of the males are active all year, but most polar bears spend a lot of time during the cold months sleeping in their den.

LONG HAIRS KEEP THE SKIN DRY AND WARM

Double layer of fur
The polar bear's double layer of fur protects it against the cold. When it fluffs up its thick coat, body heat is trapped between the two layers. If it gets too hot it can sleek the fur down, allowing heat to escape.

SHORT HAIRS PROVIDE SPACE TO TRAP AIR

Primates

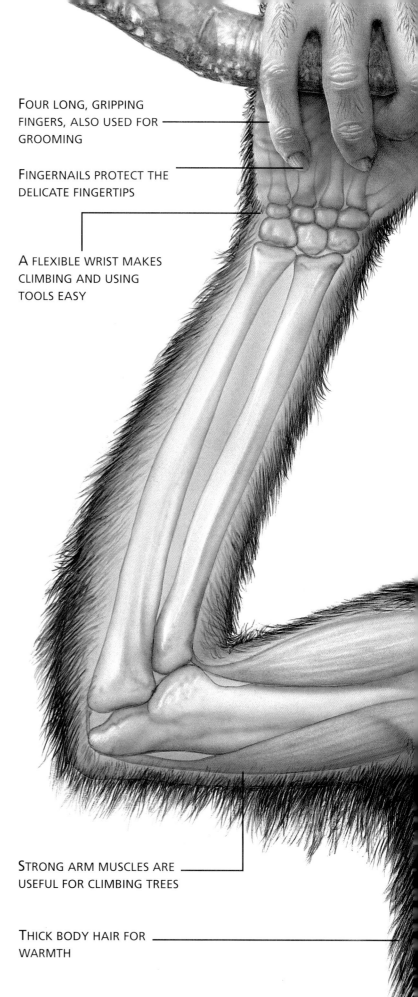

FOUR LONG, GRIPPING FINGERS, ALSO USED FOR GROOMING

FINGERNAILS PROTECT THE DELICATE FINGERTIPS

A FLEXIBLE WRIST MAKES CLIMBING AND USING TOOLS EASY

PRIMATES ARE mammals that have a very large brain. The part of the brain that thinks is especially big, making them very intelligent. Monkeys, chimpanzees, lemurs, and humans are all primates. Most primates live in the warmer parts of the world, except humans, who live in most parts.

Primates can be very big, like the gorilla, which weighs over 600 pounds. Others, like the mouse lemur, are tiny and weigh only 2 ounces. Nearly all of them are very good at climbing trees. To help them do this they have special eyes, hands, and feet. Many have a long tail, too. To communicate high in the trees primates use different sounds. Of all the primates humans make the most sounds.

①

②

③

④

STRONG ARM MUSCLES ARE USEFUL FOR CLIMBING TREES

THICK BODY HAIR FOR WARMTH

Chimp expressions
Some primates, such as chimpanzees, show their emotions through facial expressions. These include: (1) mouth closed when attacking – 'you've made me cross'; (2) mouth open to show all the teeth – 'I'm scared'; (3) mouth open, with the bottom teeth showing – 'let's play'; (4) lips pushed forward – 'give it to me'.

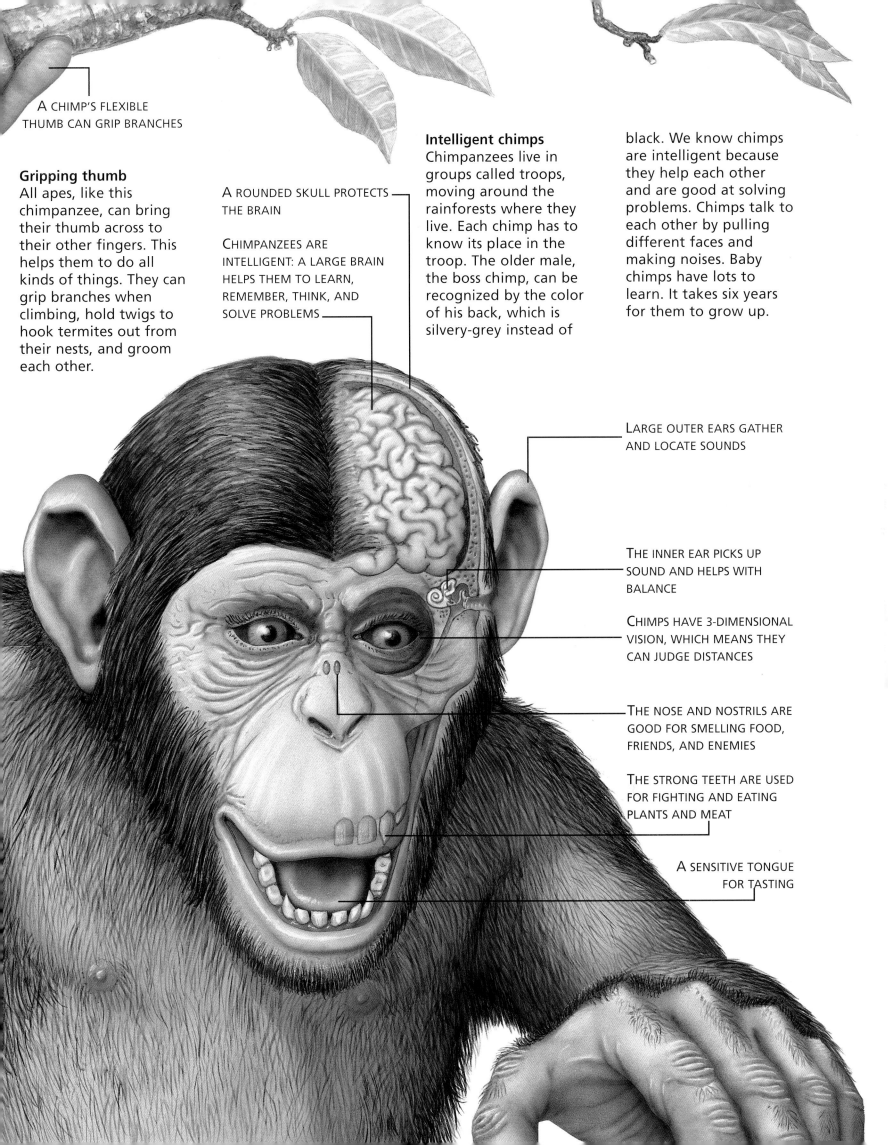

A CHIMP'S FLEXIBLE THUMB CAN GRIP BRANCHES

Gripping thumb

All apes, like this chimpanzee, can bring their thumb across to their other fingers. This helps them to do all kinds of things. They can grip branches when climbing, hold twigs to hook termites out from their nests, and groom each other.

A ROUNDED SKULL PROTECTS THE BRAIN

CHIMPANZEES ARE INTELLIGENT: A LARGE BRAIN HELPS THEM TO LEARN, REMEMBER, THINK, AND SOLVE PROBLEMS

Intelligent chimps

Chimpanzees live in groups called troops, moving around the rainforests where they live. Each chimp has to know its place in the troop. The older male, the boss chimp, can be recognized by the color of his back, which is silvery-grey instead of black. We know chimps are intelligent because they help each other and are good at solving problems. Chimps talk to each other by pulling different faces and making noises. Baby chimps have lots to learn. It takes six years for them to grow up.

LARGE OUTER EARS GATHER AND LOCATE SOUNDS

THE INNER EAR PICKS UP SOUND AND HELPS WITH BALANCE

CHIMPS HAVE 3-DIMENSIONAL VISION, WHICH MEANS THEY CAN JUDGE DISTANCES

THE NOSE AND NOSTRILS ARE GOOD FOR SMELLING FOOD, FRIENDS, AND ENEMIES

THE STRONG TEETH ARE USED FOR FIGHTING AND EATING PLANTS AND MEAT

A SENSITIVE TONGUE FOR TASTING

Community Life

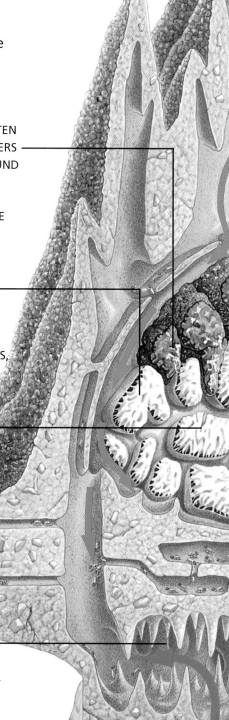

MILLIONS OF TERMITES live together in communities called colonies. Each termite does a specific job, like gathering food, looking after the young, or guarding the colony against attack. This means that termites are social insects, as each individual works towards the good of the whole colony. In such a large community, good communication is vital. The termites need to respond to problems as soon as they arise. One way termites communicate is by releasing special chemicals that other termites can smell.

Termites are pale and have soft bodies so they need to avoid dry air and sunlight. They hide away inside their nests and burrows, and only come out at night, if at all. Some termites, like the ones shown here, use soil to make very complicated nests. Others produce more simple structures inside rotting wood.

Air circulation
Millions of termites living together need plenty of fresh air to breathe. They also need to keep the air cool. So termites build their nest in such a way that the air moves through it, keeping the conditions fresh and cool. This circulating air also means that the chemical scents they use for communication will carry from one termite to another.

HOT STALE AIR RISES AND ESCAPES THROUGH THE CHIMNEYS

POROUS CHIMNEY MATERIAL DRAWS IN FRESH AIR AND RELEASES THE STALE AIR

PIECES OF PLANTS ARE EATEN AND GATHERED BY WORKERS AND TAKEN INTO THE MOUND

FUNGUS IS GROWN ON THE STORED PLANT MATERIAL. THE TERMITES EAT THE FUNGUS AND FEED IT TO THEIR YOUNG

FUNGUS PRODUCTION NEEDS TERMITE DROPPINGS, MOIST AIR, AND A PRECISE TEMPERATURE OF 30–31°C

UNDERGROUND CELLARS COOL THE AIR AND GIVE IT MOISTURE

Soldiers
Ants are the main enemy of termites. The soldier termites defend the colony from attack using their special jaws. Some bite while others use their jaws to spray a sticky glue at the attacker. Soldier termites cannot feed themselves; they are fed by the worker termites.

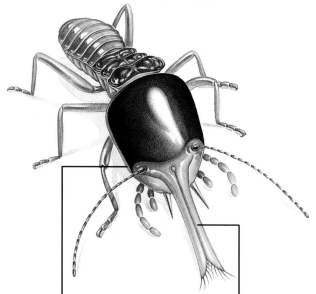

POWERFUL JAW MUSCLES ARE HOUSED IN THE LARGE HEAD

GLUE IS SPRAYED OUT THROUGH THIS TUBE

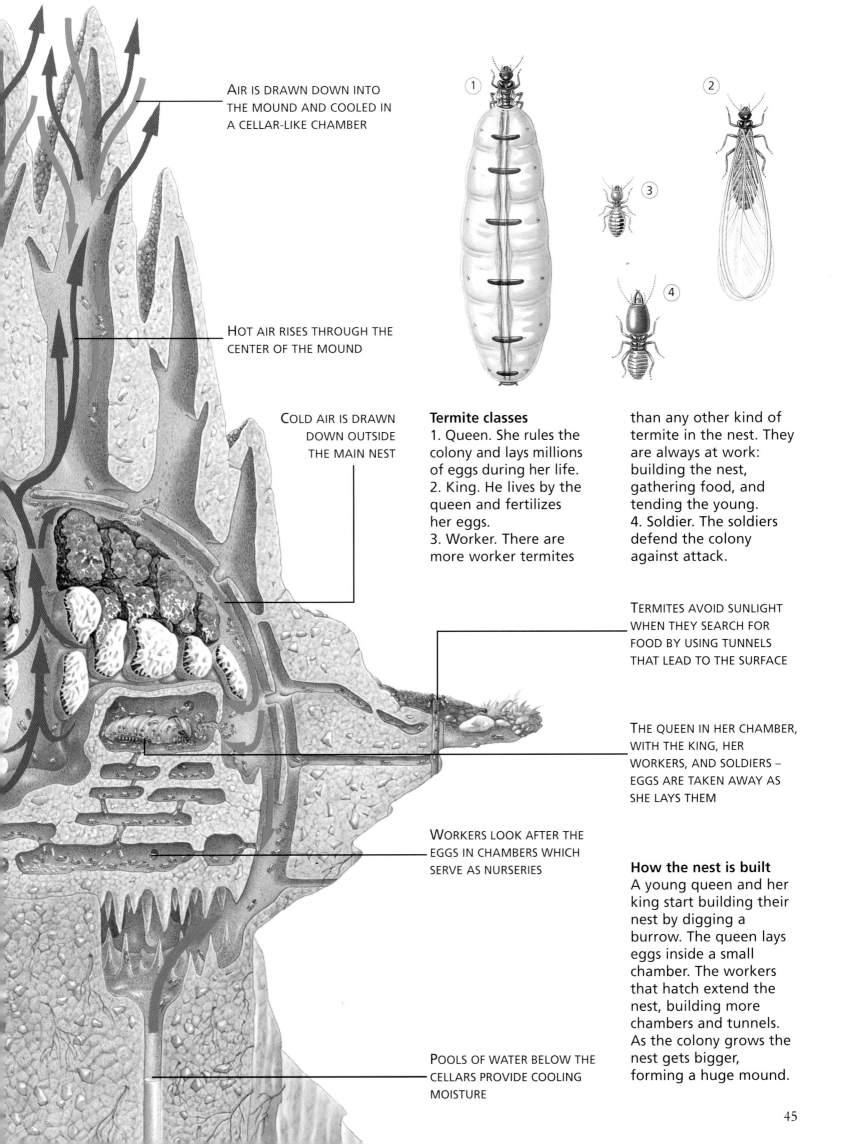

AIR IS DRAWN DOWN INTO THE MOUND AND COOLED IN A CELLAR-LIKE CHAMBER

HOT AIR RISES THROUGH THE CENTER OF THE MOUND

COLD AIR IS DRAWN DOWN OUTSIDE THE MAIN NEST

Termite classes
1. Queen. She rules the colony and lays millions of eggs during her life.
2. King. He lives by the queen and fertilizes her eggs.
3. Worker. There are more worker termites than any other kind of termite in the nest. They are always at work: building the nest, gathering food, and tending the young.
4. Soldier. The soldiers defend the colony against attack.

TERMITES AVOID SUNLIGHT WHEN THEY SEARCH FOR FOOD BY USING TUNNELS THAT LEAD TO THE SURFACE

THE QUEEN IN HER CHAMBER, WITH THE KING, HER WORKERS, AND SOLDIERS – EGGS ARE TAKEN AWAY AS SHE LAYS THEM

WORKERS LOOK AFTER THE EGGS IN CHAMBERS WHICH SERVE AS NURSERIES

How the nest is built
A young queen and her king start building their nest by digging a burrow. The queen lays eggs inside a small chamber. The workers that hatch extend the nest, building more chambers and tunnels. As the colony grows the nest gets bigger, forming a huge mound.

POOLS OF WATER BELOW THE CELLARS PROVIDE COOLING MOISTURE

Index